The Thoughts I See

By Michelle J.E. Temple

Copyright of Michelle J.E. Temple

Dedication

This book is dedicated to my ancestors who did not have the means, the technology or the societal acceptance to fight these diseases. In my family history, there is depression, schizophrenia, forms of obsessive-compulsive disorder, and other undiagnosed mental illnesses. Thinking of those who went before me who were scared and alone, with no support systems, makes me grateful to be alive in this time period, but sad that they suffered so much in silence.

To the many people who suffer today from depression, obsessive compulsive disorder, anxiety, substance abuse, as well as other mental illnesses: May we eventually accept these illnesses as we accept physical illness. For now, seek help; you are not alone. I feel you and I see you. There is so much support in so many forms that you can lead a happy, productive, loving, well-lived life.

To women past and present who have suffered with endometriosis, infertility, post-partum depression, and ischemic colitis: Keep on fighting. We have come a long way from just having to suffer through undiagnosed pelvic pain. Search for specialists. You got this!

To my husband Kevin, my daughters Kierra and Ava, and my son Brant: You are my light in the darkness. Thank you for loving me as much as I love you.

To my extended family, friends, and all my supporters: I love you, and your support keeps my light shining.

To my mom, dad, siblings and in-laws: Thank you for loving me, I wanted to protect you from the truth so you weren't hurt by my pain. I love you so much and I need to be free.

Dear Reader,

I have so much unpacking to do to tell you who I am. I am just exhausted saying all of this out loud, so I have decided to write it down.

I want to stare all of it in the face. I want to look it in the eye. I want to heal. I also want to bring awareness to chronic illness, the failing health system – for women in particular, – and myths about mental health and suicide. So, here it goes – the good, bad, the ugly, and the downright horrifying truth. I can barely admit these things in my mind, so writing them down should prove interesting.

I don't want people to look at me differently, but I guess I look at myself differently. To know me authentically would be to know that behind the laughs lie some inherently faulty chemical imbalances that have caused some major disturbances throughout my life – by far the worst being actual suicidal plans in 2023 and 2024.

I also would like to state up front that anything I say in this book about my own experience is not meant to generalize, target, judge, or demean anyone else. Whether it be mental illness, weight, chronic pain, or any other societal issues, everything I write about here is purely based on my own experiences and perceptions. I would never generalize or assume the reader shares my opinion.

So here I go: 5, 4, 3, 2, 1. . .

Prologue

In February 2024, my new therapist and I sit down in her office for our first session. Her first question is, "Who are you? Tell me everything about what makes you the person you are." I sigh, thinking, *I don't even know where to start...* This is what I am able to convey to her that first day:

> I have a terrible self-image. I have violent visions of harm being done to others and to myself. I loathe myself and I have major depression. I have periods where I see myself stabbing my legs, stomach, and head with a knife. I think I am fat, lazy, spoiled, stupid, and I say the worst things at the worst times. I am a total fake. I have smiled and laughed for the last twenty-eight years while I battled the violent images and self-loathing. I only recently admitted the truth to a psychiatrist last year.
>
> I am also a successful chartered accountant manager, the farm wife of a cattle operation, and I have been with my husband, Kevin, for thirty-one years. I have a nineteen-year-old girl, Kierra, a seventeen-year-old girl, Ava, and then there came our little afterthought, an eight-year-old boy named Brant.

She says, "Wow, that's a lot." I laugh to myself; I have only just begun.

> I also have stage four severe endometriosis that I have battled for fourteen years and ischemic colitis attacks for which I had to go to the Mayo Clinic for answers. My eyes turn yellow when I get attacks, so currently, there is an investigation of my high liver enzymes. A year and a half ago, at age forty-six, I had a complete hysterectomy, and I have no ovaries as well. I'm on add-back estrogen, and there is a change in one of my breasts that appears suspicious.

My therapist sighs. I understand her reaction.

***

In January of 2024, following a lifetime of illnesses, both mental and physical, I was referred by a psychiatrist to undergo transcranial magnetic stimulation (TMS), a newer form of what used to be known as "shock therapy." This rather drastic move was the culmination of a very long struggle with mental health. TMS is a non-invasive therapy that involves the use of a magnetic field to influence the natural electrical activity of your brain. A series of magnets are taped onto your head, creating electrical current in certain places to restore connections or "pathways" in your brain. What led to this treatment is a story of fear, suicidal thoughts, and uncontrollable recurring violent mental images. As a way of trying to understand what has made me "the person I am" as my therapist said, I have recently reflected a lot on my past.

My life is in many ways typical, and in many ways unique. For the most part, I had a wonderful, idyllic childhood, filled with all the fun that could have been had in the late seventies and early eighties. What a great time to be a kid! We were free to roam the neighborhood together, wearing stirrup pants and mullets and listening to Michael Jackson. I had a lot of love from my parents, siblings, and extended family. Besides some teasing that is to be expected among kids, I can't complain about anything in particular that would have limited me from achieving my full potential.

I am the baby of the family—my oldest brother, Kelly, is nine years older than me, my sister, Wanda, is eight years older, and my brother Ron is seven years older. We had enough money, we travelled and went camping, and we had lots of family events, which I loved! My mom and dad are wonderful people, kind and caring, and my childhood was filled with warmth and family events.

Growing up, I was aware of the mental health issues that some of my aunts and uncles suffered, and it always scared me that I might end up like them one day. I remember doing a book report on schizophrenia at a very young age, and a point that always stuck with me was that there was a nine percent chance that I would have it.

One relative in particular became a beacon of fear, both for my immediate safety and for what it might mean for me in the future. This was my uncle, who lived across the street from us during my childhood. He was confirmed to have schizophrenia, and became a kind of bogey man for me as a child. Although he was always nice to me, he had a terrible and unexpected temper. One time some of the older kids in town were teasing him. He came out on his front step hollering, and he had a gun. My friend and I saw the whole thing because we were outside eating supper. We quickly grabbed our plates and ran up to my room to call my parents. I think he was reported to the police that night and at least some of his guns were taken away.

I also had an aunt with schizophrenia. When I was in elementary school she went into a decline, eventually becoming completely disabled. I remember as a child visiting her at the mental health hospital. She wasn't violent like my uncle, but she always said strange things – she wasn't paranoid, but she was childlike, saying inappropriate things and being very loud about it. As I became an adolescent, we would take her out sometimes, and she would completely embarrass me. I felt bad that I was so ashamed of her, but I also felt guilty if I didn't accompany Mom on the outings.

My own mental health journey began after high school. As a child I experienced nothing out of the ordinary, and my mind was relatively quiet and calm. Although I never tapped into my creativity a lot until I was older, I was very good in school – not amazing, but I didn't have to work to learn. I feel like I could always visualize concepts like numbers and maps in my mind, like a bunch of photographs.

When I graduated high school, I decided I would go to the University of Regina, and in my first year I lived with my sister, cousin and a friend. Like any early experience with roommates, we went through the usual trials, but I think being with family made the transition to living away from home easier.

The following year, I started a co-op program, which was a job placement setup where I worked for four months and then went to school for four months in alternation. I got a job at Ford Credit Canada. At that time, I lived with a friend in a basement apartment. My boyfriend, Kevin, was working at a mine two hours from the city. For some reason, this was the first time in my life I experienced real loneliness. When my roommate would go home on the weekend and Kevin was working, I remember feeling so alone, not knowing what to do with myself. Should I go shopping by myself? Go to the park? I had an overwhelming sense of sadness, and I wasn't sure where it came from.

Around that time, something frightening started happening. I began seeing horrific images everywhere I looked. I would walk down the street and see people being stabbed and gutted in front of me. I would see pregnant mothers being kicked repeatedly, and babies having their heads cut off. The violent images would go on to haunt me throughout my life, sometimes tapering off, but always returning sooner or later. At some points, there would be so many in one minute and then none the next. But slowly I managed to get some control over it, and the time between the images spread farther apart. In fact, I had great success with finishing my degree. I got my Chartered Accountant designation and Kevin and I got married. We even went on a year-and-a-half adventure to Australia to work for an accounting firm there. It wasn't until I had my first baby at twenty-eight years old that I would again go down into the depths of seeing horrific images.

Around thirty-five years old, I began to struggle with debilitating abdominal pains that would come and go. They were so painful they would take my breath away. They went undiagnosed for many years. I was referred to my gynecologist in 2016 as the pains were relentless and felt like a knife being stabbed repeatedly in my lower abdomen. He discovered I had a cyst on one of my ovaries. Because of its size, which was like a small orange, he decided to do surgery. In June 2017, I had the operation, thinking they were just going to remove the cyst and that would be it.

When I woke up from surgery, I remember being alone and feeling very high; however, I wasn't in recovery – I was in a regular hospital room, which didn't make sense. The nurses told me there were complications with my surgery, so I was staying the night. I was a little dumbfounded when the doctor came to tell me that he was very surprised to find the cyst was a large endometrioma, and that my insides were like a "crow's nest." According to him, my organs were all tied together – my bowel, bladder, and uterus – with tight strings. He ended up having to remove my one ovary because it wound so tightly with the endometrioma that there was no way to get them separated. He said I had stage four endometriosis, or what they call "frozen pelvis." At that moment, I began a journey that paralleled the one I was on with my mental health, trying to diagnose and treat the full extent of what was causing the ongoing worsening pelvic pain.

    This book is my attempt to chronicle that journey in the hopes that others who suffer in similar ways will be able to benefit from it. I want my struggle to serve a greater purpose, and hope that anyone reading this who is questioning what to do or how to get through it can take strength from me and my story.

TMS Referral

The referral for transcranial magnetic stimulation came as a result of a particularly traumatic day in January. I had been plagued with violent images of self-harm since the Christmas holidays, and they were increasing. My psychiatrist had recently put me on an antipsychotic, Ziprasidone, which I was taking in addition to my antidepressant. Three days after beginning the medication I had a therapy appointment during my lunch hour from work. This was the same therapist I had been seeing for sixteen years. For the first time ever, all I did during the session was cry. My therapist told me I needed to "pick myself up" and reassure myself that the images I was seeing were not real. His advice frustrated me, and I told him so. I said that I was getting tired of fighting. I told him that I was scared that the voices in my head would eventually tell me to do something horrible and I would comply.

"Remember what we've talked about," he said reassuringly. "Tell the thoughts, 'You are not me.' Look at them as something happening in your brain, but not real."

"I don't think that's going to work," I replied. "The thoughts *are* me."

He shook his head. "No, they aren't. You must remember who is in control."

I was becoming more frustrated. "What if I fall into psychosis and hurt someone, or actually follow through with my suicidal thoughts?" I was nearly in tears. "Tell me this won't happen again, that I will come out of this alright."

He smiled at me. "All you can do is wait for the medication to take effect. It might be a couple of weeks before you feel better, but you'll get there."

I returned to work in tears. As I sat down at my desk, I realized I had forgotten a meeting with my boss that was due to begin any minute. I was flustered and tried to begin the video call with him, complete with red puffy eyes and a flushed face. I had recently moved into a new office and had not put up any pictures on the walls, so they were a stark white behind me.

His first words to me were, "Well it looks like you are in an institution!"

I laughed and thought to myself, *You have no idea how spot on you are right now.* I decided it was a good time to confide in him about my struggle, since at that moment my emotions were at a level ten.

"So how are things going with you?" he asked.

"Well, I've learned something today – don't have therapy appointments on your lunch break!" I said with a laugh.

He chuckled a bit, but I could tell he knew there was going to be more to the story. I told him a little about my struggles with mental health, giving him a brief outline about what was happening. He was very understanding, and reassured me that this was not unusual. After sharing some anecdotes from his experiences with others and giving me some helpful advice, he ended the meeting on a very positive note.

"I want you to know that any time you feel like you need a break, don't hesitate to take one. Everyone needs a mental health day from time to time. When you need it, you can have it, no questions asked."

I thanked him and we signed off. I tried to work after the call, but something kept stirring inside of me. The therapist conversation, the boss conversation, the feeling that I was heading out of control…I realized I needed to act. I got up from my desk, but didn't know what to do. I could feel the anxiety rising inside me.

My first thought was to text my friend Shelly.

Can I come to your house? I asked her. I felt like I needed to be among friends and family.

I'm on my way home. Plans at 7:00 but we can meet before? Is everything ok? she responded.

I just needed to get somewhere safe. I wasn't quite ready to outright ask for help, so I texted *I was just finishing up work and to never mind, it's ok. I'll just head home and pick up supper for the fam.*

I thought ok good, now Shelly thinks I am home and I'll text Kevin that I am going to Shelly's so no one knows where I am or is expecting me. Now I'll have time to myself and then this feeling of making me want to make plans to end my life will work.

Or maybe I should just get to the hospital, I'm scared. These don't feel like my own thoughts again.

Shelly texted again, *I just got home, come over.*

I texted Shelly again: *Ok, I'll come over I think I just need to eat. I don't feel like myself.*

I then texted Kevin to tell him what was going on, and to ask him to make sure I got to her house. But then I started to feel an elevated panic, my hands shaking, my heart beating fast. I had an overwhelming fear that I was losing my own voice in these thoughts, which were telling me to make a plan to commit suicide.

I texted Shelly again: *Never mind I think I'll just go straight to the hospital; I don't feel safe with myself.*

Immediately my phone rang, and she said, "I'll come to your work and bring you some food and then we will figure it out ok?"

As I waited outside for her in the office parking lot, I thought about getting in my car and running away, go finish your plan my mind was telling me. Just as I was about to get in my car, she pulled up. "Get in, I brought you blueberries, bananas, and some nuts for protein, sorry it's all I had" she said in an apologetic rushed tone.

She talked to me for a while, and we discussed going to the hospital and I kept wavering if I need to and what were they really going to do anyways? One time in ER when my pain was so severe, and I said I wanted to smash my head in a wall. After that comment they asked about my mental state. The staff told me to stop making fun and offered me a pamphlet on depression. I felt that was the extent of the care I would get again but this time I had Shelly to be my advocate. I knew I still just didn't feel right. My heart was pounding, thoughts racing.

When we arrived at the hospital, we went into triage pretty much immediately and they said it was going to be a long wait to see a doctor. I looked at Shelly and said "forget it, we are going home." The nurse and her both said at the same time "no you are not."

While we waited I tried to think of ways to get away from Shelly and get back to my car at the office. Once I went to get a bottle of water from the entrance drink machine and felt it was my time to run, luckily for me it was -30 outside and I knew it was too cold for me to run the mile back to my car.

Another time I went to throw up in the bathroom as I was feeling so agitated that I had to vomit and when I was in the bathroom I was thinking of other ways I could get away from Shelly. Finally, I sat down in the waiting room chair and after a while I fell into a bit of a sleep which seemed to re-set where my brain was at. Shelly seemed to even look at me different when I started talking like I was sounding more like myself. I told her then how I wanted to run away from her earlier, we laughed and she said "if I tried it again, security would be on me so fast I wouldn't have very far to run."

At that point it seemed like a short wait, and they called us in to see the doctor. He gave me some Ativan to calm me down, then had us wait some more until he could reach my psychiatrist. Eventually it was decided that they would take me off the Ziprasidone and put me on a new medication, Seroquel. But during the conversation about switching medicine, the doctor let it slip that my psychiatrist had said we were "running out of options."

Shelly was shocked he said that out loud. "Why did he have to say 'out of options?" she said after he left the room. "Who says that to a suicidal patient?" Shelly shook her head.

Thankfully for me, the Ativan was kicking in fast. I let the comment slide and soon Shelly was driving me home. I was feeling relaxed, very tired, and ready for sleep.

The calm didn't last. I slept for a while that night, but around four a.m., I got up and went into the kitchen. I wandered around, then got my phone and started googling. I looked up how much medicine it would take for me to overdose. I felt compelled to do it, so that I would be prepared when I eventually decided to go through with it. I felt more and more like I was not in control, and the bad thoughts were taking over my decision-making abilities.

Over the next few days, I struggled in and out of these suicidal ideations. In the bathtub I put my head under the water and waited for a bit, visualizing what it would be like to drown. Then I sat up, realizing I didn't want to be found like that. I thought about my children and how devastated my middle child would be to lose me before she graduated. This led to the most awful thoughts. I had read about a man in Calgary who killed his wife and two children before killing himself. I reasoned that he must have snapped, then decided to take them with him so they wouldn't be sad and miss him.

Luckily at that moment I was aware enough to realize I was in trouble. Kevin was out doing chores, and I quickly texted him to come in the house right away. The direction of my thoughts scared me so much that it physically felt like it hurt my heart. We phoned the psychiatrist's office and were able to get an appointment that afternoon.

When we got there, I told my doctor all I had been going through. "I'm just so tired of it, I want to scream. I feel so defeated. I have tried and tried and tried. What do I have to do? What does this life want from me? I just want to be here and be happy and enjoy my life. Why won't it leave me alone?"

I had forgiven him for the "out of options" comment. Now I just needed him to help me.

He folded his hands on the desk and looked at me. "Well, I think it may be time to take your treatment in a different direction," he said. "Have you ever heard of transcranial magnetic stimulation?"

Kevin and I looked at each other. "No," I replied. "What's that?"

We soon found out. I was to start tomorrow and bypass the waitlist. I would have 40 days of treatments, 5 days a week, with 2 each day, so a total of 80.

TMS Session One

The next day I found myself in a treatment room, about to begin the process. I was worried about the pain, because I had heard it hurt a lot in the beginning. But the psychiatrist had told me he'd never had someone quit because of it, and that he'd seen a lot of success in his patients who suffered with depression and OCD. I was ready to do anything just to feel better.

The technician talked me through the process. I sat down in a comfortable chair that had a velvet black cushion that I could choose to hold if I would like during the treatment. First I had to remove my rings, I always wear two that I never remove, my wedding ring and my anniversary ring. Then I had to take out my nose ring and make sure I had no earrings or necklace or other jewelry on. Then the helmet that would send the magnetic pulses was placed on my head and strapped to my chin. I had previously been told to come up with a "script" that I would use during the treatment. In the first segment, I was to try to focus on positive things from my past. During the second part, I would try to call up negative things to trigger my brain into a reaction. In this way the idea was to trace old pathways in my brain and then rebuild new ones that would eventually become fixed and allow me to change how I react to stimuli and triggers.

I can't even describe how painful the first ten minutes of the first treatment were. There was a magnet hit to my brain every eight seconds. My eye twitched, my teeth chattered, my hands and feet jumped, and the tears started to flow. I honestly didn't think I would ever make it through the session. But soon thoughts started to come up, memories from my childhood. I was intrigued, and although the pain continued and I kept crying, my thoughts were occupied.

I was in the house of a friend of the family who I called my Aunt Elaine. I used to visit this house a lot as a child. But now the house was empty. As the magnets hit, I saw every detail in the empty house. I felt like a young child wandering around, and I really didn't feel scared or upset. It just felt so empty and sad. I saw it all in great detail, remembering where everything used to be. I saw the toy room, which had a piano in it, and so many toys. One in particular that I remembered was a yellow plastic bouncer that threw out balls when you pressed on the top. I walked into every room and imagined what used to be there. I tried pressing myself during these thoughts to see if anything bad had happened, but I couldn't remember. But I did recall that I have had many dreams about this house through the years. Nothing bad happens in the dreams, but seeing it now made me wonder why I dream about it so often. I made a mental note to research later why this house had so much meaning for me.

When the first part of the treatment was done, I had to stimulate my brain for the second segment by reading my script that I had prepared ahead of time. This script consisted of all the awful thoughts and images that I could think of that had been plaguing me. The idea is that by reading the script, I would trigger them to come alive in my head so I could relive them during therapy.

This treatment was not as physically painful as the first one; what hurt more was repeatedly going over my triggers and experiencing the imagery over and over again. I began to see all the horrific images I used to see: people disemboweled before my eyes, pregnant women and babies being tortured. I was so scared, I pleaded with myself to make the images stop, but they would just get worse. I remembered killers I had obsessed over. There was a little girl who had been assaulted and killed by a man and woman, and I couldn't get the case out of my mind. Her name was Victoria Stafford, she was eight years old, and she was abducted and murdered by a man and a woman on her way home from school. I thought about Paul Bernardo, a violent serial rapist who, along with his fiancée Karla Homolka, had raped and killed Karla's younger sister, then later killed two more young schoolgirls, dismembering one of them with a power saw. I couldn't stop seeing the dead bodies. Then I remembered one time when I was young and had been out for lunch with my family and started seeing garbage bags everywhere that were full of body parts. No matter where we walked, I had to keep picking my way around pieces of hands, legs, arms, hair, heads. In my mind I saw myself getting more garbage bags and putting the body parts in them. I remember feeling like I had to figure out how I was going to get rid of all the evidence.

When it was over I was physically and mentally exhausted. The technician unstrapped the helmet and I put my jewelry back on. I was so shaken, and the technician very kindly looked me right in the eyes and said "that was for therapy it is over now and you don't have to think about it for the rest of the day." I got home and had to rest and recover from the treatment. Later that night, I decided to message my siblings and talk on the phone to my parents and let them know I was going for this therapy. This was the first time I had ever talked to my parents about my struggles. They were very supportive and thanked me for sharing what I was going through. I decided it was a good time to ask about their friend, Aunt Elaine's house and its significance to me. Mom said that we were there a lot in my childhood, and we always had a lot of fun. Whether we were playing cards or making perogies, I always loved going over there. She also said that she remembered how difficult it had been for me years later when Aunt Elaine passed away. I was an adult by that time, but she said she knew how sad I was that my aunt wouldn't be at my wedding, which was the following year. My sister confirmed this on the phone the next day, and said that Aunt Elaine had really loved us in a way that was almost like another parent. I wondered if maybe I never did deal with the grief of losing her, and that seeing the empty house was my mind's way of looking for her as if I were a child.

Another big piece of the puzzle I talked to my parents about was my schizophrenic uncle. I used to be so afraid of him, and I worried that one night he would snap and come in our house and kill us all. They were shocked that I was even aware of the fear everyone had about him. I told them how I remembered that a lot of his rage was directed at Dad. Once he was convinced that Dad was giving information about him to airplanes, and that they were coming to get him. He said that he knew Dad was to blame. I remembered another instance one Halloween when we were all dressed up and out trick or treating. My dad was wearing a really funny mask, like a clown or an animal. We happened to walk by my uncle's house and he came outside, thinking we were the neighbor kids out to get him. He jumped on Dad and started punching him. I can still see the rage in his eyes as Mom screamed at him to stop. He finally stopped for a second, giving Dad time to rip his mask off, and thankfully he recognized him and calmed down. We didn't go out trick or treating anymore as a family. I would go with my friends but never near my uncle's house.

    My parents told me they could never forget that night. Mom said he had also hollered at her a lot in the car when I was little, but I don't remember that. They also admitted that they too felt like he might snap, and that if he did, we would be his first targets. It confirmed for me that the fear of that particular uncle was not just real in my little inner child's mind, but that it was a very real threat to everyone involved.

TMS Session Two

On the second day of treatment, I continued to bring up memories of my early childhood. During the first half of the session, where I was supposed to reflect on positive thoughts, I thought about family vacations and how much I used to enjoy them. I saw Dad making bacon and eggs over a campfire on a camping trip, while mom made coffee in her old percolator. I remembered that she had told us she'd had that percolator for a long time, since their wedding. I could smell the coffee and the lake air around me as I came out of the camper to join them for breakfast. Then I saw other family get togethers – ball games, more camping trips, and holidays. I remembered that once on vacation, my aunt Elaine started a water fight and we all got soaked. They were all great memories.

However, the reality was that childhood wasn't all good. My mind went back to when I moved schools to what I considered the big city. My hometown had a population of about 70 people total, and the big city had 5000, so it was a big city to me! In my hometown we had a two-room schoolhouse, with grade one to three in one room and grade four to six in the other. I felt a bit like a loser coming from this small school to a big school. I tried to make myself some promises: when I get there, I am going to be cool, I'm going to find the popular kids and I'm going to fit in. But the truth was that most people from my hometown didn't fit in.

I got dressed for my first day of school. I had short hair, glasses, and was a bit on the chubby side. I picked out some acid-wash jeans and a dress shirt, with some weird pink-patterned cardigan. I also wore long pink pearls that I tied in a knot. Off I went!

It didn't take me long to figure out that I was, in fact, not a cool kid at all. In my mind, I was just a loser from a small town.. I remember one day in school a note was being passed around and everyone was laughing. I later found out that the note said something like *That weird bead girl is such a loser!* I made a mental note: no more wearing pearls or beads, and no more trying to fit in. I was awkward and everyone knew it. I still played with Barbies and Cabbage Patch Kids, and the only things I saw of the real world were movies that my older siblings watched. I had no idea how to be a teenager.

But I tried to find things to get involved in. I thought maybe I would try out for the volleyball team, even though I had never played volleyball before. I told Mom about it and she didn't say much besides, "Okay, when do I pick you up?"

I should also add that I was not good at sports. I was always picked last on every team, from childhood through high school. I never got any ribbons in anything besides participation, except for one event…the tire roll! In that event, each participant got a regular-sized tire and had to roll it to the other side in a race. For some reason, fate had given me a blue ribbon in that race. It became an ongoing family joke that the only thing I was good at was the tire roll. So, I'm sure it will not be too shocking for you to learn that I did not make the volleyball team in grade seven!

Eventually, I started talking to girls who were my partners in science, and slowly I began to make connections. I found that one way to get attention was to be silly. I would sing out loud and do chair races in the hall. It would get me in trouble, but that made me cooler.

I did end up making friends, but I don't think that I felt like I ever measured up to them and their coolness. They were pretty and they dated hockey players, and I was a bit frumpy and was no guy's first choice, and I knew that. They seemed to form bonds over their hockey-player boyfriends, and I sat out. Later when I met Kevin, I spent more time with him and less with the girls from school and outed myself a bit from being in the core group of the popular girls and guys. Even later at university, I was further isolated because I had my boyfriend back home. Eventually I met a whole new group of friends, and we have remained close my whole life.

During the second half of the TMS session, like the day before, I was supposed to read my script and let myself get agitated. For some reason, this time I found myself using the pain of the treatment as a way to punish myself. I thought of all the reasons I hated myself, and then every time the magnet hit, it felt good, because it was an act of aggression against myself. I told myself that I was so dumb for starting to tell people about my mental struggle! People would think I was crazy now and not trust me with anything! My mind started to spiral: I was fat, I was lazy, I was disgusting.

As I let myself feel these thoughts, I started to realize the impact my obsession with weight had had on me, starting when I was in school. My relationship with food had always been unhealthy, and weight was something that I had struggled with for as long as I remember. I used food as a reward, to soothe my soul, to suppress my emotions, and to experience joy. When I was young, probably about grade six or seven, I started to gain some weight. At the time, Mom had decided to go on a diet for herself, and she put me on it as well. I honestly don't remember if it was her idea or mine. She also encouraged me to go walking with her on her usual two-mile route. There was nothing wrong with her wanting to get me out to get some exercise, but the guilt I felt if I didn't go on those walks was overpowering. And the diets were always strange. For example, one diet we were on called for a different food every day of the week, and you could only eat that, nothing else. Sardines and water were one day, milk and bananas another. I also remember pita bread and milk day, and the taste of warm milk from my lunch box. I hated it! Anytime I was alone, I would go to the cupboard that had the treats, chips, chocolate, Twizzlers, and other snacks, and I would eat them in my closet upstairs. When I got a little older, I would go for a run and throw them up.

In high school, I was a little overweight, probably around 140 pounds on my five-foot-four-inch body. To me, I was huge, and I assumed that my weight was the reason boys didn't like me. In grade 11, I started to really work out. I'd wake up early in the morning, do aerobics, eat healthy, and I lost weight. I was so proud of myself, and when I looked in the mirror, I saw someone who was starting to look worthy of attracting boys. One party I went to, I was told that three different guys were interested in me. However, I had interest in someone else, who, of course, wasn't interested in me. He told me that night that he didn't want to go out with me. On the way home from the party, I played a FireHouse cassette tape in my Dodge Daytona, singing loudly, "Baby don't treat me bad; I could be the best thing that you ever had." I was heartbroken. I still didn't feel like I was good enough.

When I went to university, I again started to pack on a few pounds from beer, beer, and more beer. I struggled on and off – my weight went up and my weight went down. Finally, I started going to the gym, eating plain chicken breast and rice, and not eating sweets. My weight went down, and I thought I was looking pretty good. I got a fair amount of attention from guys at the bar, so I seemed to be on the right track.

After graduation, I was probably back up to 140 pounds. I didn't like looking in the mirror and seeing my big butt, so I started a hard-core diet. I remember forcing myself to have 600 calories a day. I would head off to work with my 0% fat and sugar yoghurt and Nutribar breakfast. For lunch, I would grab straight white rice with a wee bit of red sauce. In the afternoon, I would have a diet cherry Pepsi. For supper, I would have some plain chicken breast and vegetables, including lots of cucumbers. I started to lose weight again, thank goodness. I lost weight fairly quickly and soon I reached 125 pounds. When I saw photos of myself, I loved the way I looked. Yep! That was the girl who was pretty! That was the girl who was attractive! But I still wasn't thin enough.

***

When session two of TMS ended, I felt like I was beginning to see myself clearly for the first time. On the way home I began to make a connection I hadn't thought of before. Back when I worked as a co-op student at Ford Credit, there were some older women I worked with who made me very upset on a daily basis. They would tease me about my skirt being too short or my top too low. They treated me like I was a terrible worker, insinuating that I was just some bimbo who had lucked into the job instead of a university student with intelligence and talent. I realized that this had been the moment that the violent images started. The more they teased me, the harder I got on myself, and the more I saw the violent images. So, it seems that the images were directly linked to my self-hatred. I don't know if I had it all my life or if it came on gradually. But the more they snubbed me, the more I saw the violent images, and the more I saw the images, the more and more I hated myself.

Maybe even as I write this, I'm being hard on myself. In reality, I do have some faulty chemical imbalances and lack of blood flow to parts of my brain, and I am genetically wired to have OCD and depression. Maybe it isn't fair to come up with the reasons why I hate myself.

An acquaintance recently said to me, "You have everything, a nice house, amazing farm, good looking husband, beautiful children, a big happy family…how on earth could you be depressed?"

I responded, "Well, I'm getting them to hit my brain with magnets to try to find out!"

Maybe I'm looking at every life event trying to find an answer, trying to discover when I started hating myself. Maybe I won't find it because maybe it is just a disease. Could self-hate be a disease?

TMS Session Three

On the third day, again I focused on good memories for the first part of treatment. This time I centered on when Kevin and I were first dating, and all those fun times. We met when I was in grade 12. I had been losing weight at the time, and had grown my hair long. I would look in the mirror and think, *Hey, not too bad.* In November I went to a rodeo with a friend. I saw Kevin standing across the way with a group of friends on the other side of the arena. I kept glancing over at him throughout the night. He was wearing Levis and boots and looked super cute with his curly mullet. When the rodeo was over, my friend and I were standing in the foyer of the auditorium, discussing what we were going to do next.

Kevin came walking up. "Hi, I'm wondering if you were looking at me or one of my friends."

I decided to play it cool, and replied, "I wasn't looking at any of you."

My friend snickered behind me.

"Well, do you want to go for coffee?" he then asked.

Of course I accepted. We went to A & W for coffee, and then my friend and I went for a cruise down a back road with him and a friend of his. At one point someone had a spontaneous idea to have a dance on the backroad to the song from the band Alabama, "I'm in a Hurry." It was magical. We were together from that point on.

By the time I graduated from university, Kevin and I thought we had it all figured out. I had majored in accounting and gotten a job at Crown Life, and Kevin was still working at the mine. He had finally determined at the age of twenty-five that it was time to move out of his parents' house, and he had an apartment in Esterhazy. At the time I thought we would either end up both working in Regina or we would move to somewhere like Fort McMurray, where we would work for one of the oil companies. I was twenty-one and we had been dating for four and a half years, so I was eager to move on and get our life going.

Then life threw us its first curve ball. Kevin and I had been fighting off and on for a short while. One weekend we went to Craven, an outdoor music festival. We planned to stay in a camper, as most people did, and I was excited about the trip, even though I had heard that the festival sometimes got really crazy. I had always been the kind of person who could drink my fair share of alcohol, but I didn't stay out late, and was usually ready to go home and go to sleep fairly early. Kevin, on the other hand, liked to party all night. The first night, as usual, I was ready to go back to the camper much earlier than he was. He was not happy with me, and decided to stay out while I went to bed. I was okay with that, as I did love my sleep.

The next morning, he was acting a little off, I wasn't quite sure what the vibe was that I was getting from him, but it wasn't good. Eventually he confessed to me that he had been drunk and dancing and apparently had kissed another girl. I was devastated. We broke up. I was heartbroken, and cried for weeks.

Then the next event occurred that changed the path of our lives. Kevin's fifty-year-old dad was chasing a bull through the bush and got stung by a swarm of bees. He had known that he was possibly allergic, due to a reaction he'd had years before, and he had some pills at his house. But in a matter of minutes, before he could get home, his neck swelled up and he started having trouble breathing. Kevin phoned me from the hospital and told me about the accident. He said that he'd had a chance to talk with his dad and to share with him some things he had been feeling about the farm and how hard his dad worked. When Kevin told me that he had talked to him, I assumed he was still alive, but that wasn't the case. He had been rushed to the hospital, but he didn't make it. Even so, Kevin said he told him what he wanted to tell him, even though he was already gone. He seemed satisfied that he had made peace with his dad.

I knew instinctively that I needed to be by Kevin during this unimaginably difficult week. I loved his mom, sisters and niece as well and I couldn't stay away.

We got back together. Kevin took over farming responsibilities to get things finished for his mom and I got a job in a neighboring city at an accounting firm. So, the course of our life completely changed in that moment, and we ended up going in a completely different direction to what I had anticipated.

***

The first half of the session was complete. I geared up for the second part of treatment, and read my script. I wanted to focus again on the violent images I see so often. As I said, these images began early on. One episode I remember in particular was just after I had my first child. She was born via C-section, and I remember holding my beautiful baby girl in my arms, and how happy I was to have her. My mom had been a great help during the first few weeks of being home with the baby, but had decided to go to British Columbia for a couple of weeks. I thought I was fine with her leaving, but as I told her goodbye, I realized I wasn't. I didn't cry until she drove away, but then I went downstairs to the laundry room and cried and cried. I wasn't sure why, but I knew I wasn't holding up well.

I had been having some strange experiences ever since the baby was born. My eyes would get blurry for no reason, and then I would see terrible things happening to my baby. This was different to my earlier violent images, which always involved strangers, or sometimes even anonymous body parts. Now it was focused on my newborn child. For example, if I saw a curtain with a string hanging from it, I would imagine the string wrapped around my baby's neck, her little face and body all blue, and I would scream. If I saw a knife, I would imagine it being plunged into her little body.

While I could maybe handle seeing strangers being ravaged and murdered, this was different. I felt like I couldn't take it. This was my beautiful baby. So in order to deal with it, I began to refocus the images. I would imagine the horrible things happening to me instead of my baby. Every time I saw a violent image, I would turn it on myself. If I saw a knife, I would take it and plunge it into my stomach, my neck, my ears, my brain – anywhere as long as it didn't touch her. If I saw a rope, I would immediately hang myself with it so that it wouldn't hurt her. If I saw water, I would drown myself in it to keep her safe. This started a pattern where I thought, *At least I can control these images by trying to kill myself, and she will be okay*. I thought this was the way to handle it. I told no one about it, and didn't go anywhere for help.

So, for the first six months of my daughter's life, these were my constant thoughts – hour by hour, minute by minute. It makes me sad to this day that I missed so much of her first year while I dealt with these thoughts. I wish I could go back and hold that baby girl again and experience the bliss that I was supposed to feel.

Eventually the images started to subside, and I felt better. But after our second baby was born, it all started up again. At times, I would sit almost comatose staring at the wall, trying to envision how to keep going without giving in to the suicidal thoughts that were constantly in my head. I expanded the possibilities – putting poison in a water bottle, downing a bottle of pills, and of course, the obvious ones like the rope and the knife. These thoughts took such a strong hold over me that I knew I needed to get help. I ended up calling a health line, and after a good conversation, I agreed to tell Kevin what was happening.

After I told Kevin about feeling sad, which I felt was all I could tell him at the time, we decided that I would go to my doctor to discuss postpartum depression. He had a kind heart, and talked to me for a moment, then swiftly wrote me a prescription for the antidepressant Fluoxetine. I also started going to therapy. I was able to talk to the therapist about some of what I was seeing and feeling, but I did not describe all of it. In fact, I still don't know that I can even tell myself all of it.

Fluoxetine helped a lot; it subsided the horrific images and made my mind much more peaceful. When I went off it, I seemed to be okay again for a while, and that's when I got pregnant with our accidental baby. I carried this baby for only thirteen weeks, but felt the joy of anticipating another child. I couldn't wait for the girls to have a brother or sister. Although it was a short time frame, it was long enough for me to get my head completely set on having this baby, and I was convinced that this was the way my life would play out. Except it didn't.

One day at work, I felt the blood rush down my legs. I got myself to the hospital, was given an ultrasound, and saw that my baby had no heartbeat. Kevin was in the field and not answering his phone, and I was all alone. I was devastated. After ten hours of labor, I was given a D and C and sent home. My baby that I had dreamed of was now gone, nothing but discarded fluid and tissue. I felt like more than my insides had been ripped out of me.

Then, of course, my thoughts started to spiral again. I began to obsess about poor Tori Stafford. I had read that after the man and woman abducted her, they took her into some woods and the man sexually assaulted her. A particularly horrific detail of the crime that stuck in my head was that he had let her go for a moment so she could urinate, and then brought her back and continued raping her. Afterwards they hit her in the head with a rock and hammer to kill her.

I must have seen that image thousands and thousands of times. I could never go pee out in the farm in the field or at the side of road without thinking of that little girl. It's probably been ten years and that association has still never left me. I couldn't take what they did to her, I couldn't understand it – especially the woman involved in it. I could constantly hear that little girl's screams. The images of her dying moments were so prevalent in my mind that I forced myself to turn my thoughts to suicide instead of going down that path again. My therapist recommended I write the little girl a letter to tell her how sorry I was for what happened to her. I went back to my doctor and asked for help, and was able to stabilize myself with Fluoxetine and therapy.

So, after three days of TMS, I realized that my own trauma was directly related to my obsession with other people's – specifically children's – suffering. The violent images in my mind came from my reaction to the violence in the world outside. I didn't fully understand it, but I knew that my healing would have to come from me continuing to do the work that needed to be done. I didn't believe I could be healthy until I stared those demons straight in the face.

TMS Session Four

On the fourth day of TMS, I started to look back on my pain journey. It seemed to me that a lot of my mental issues were tied in with my physical well-being. Not long after the miscarriage, I began experiencing severe stomach issues and pain. I would get cramps that would knock me to my knees, as well as diarrhea that would force me to camp out on the bathroom floor for hours and hours. During that time, there were more questions than answers regarding where these pains were coming from. They were debilitating, though I couldn't find any rhyme or reason.

One story that stands out to me the most is from a Christmas holiday we took when our girls were little. Kierra was six and Ava was four. My entire twenty-plus extended family had gathered in Palm Springs, California to celebrate. I had chosen all the presents for the girls and packaged them so carefully. I prayed that the airline wouldn't lose the luggage containing its precious cargo! We all piled into the rental house to celebrate.

But on Christmas morning, cramps and diarrhea gave me a rude wake up call. I stepped over the girls sleeping on the floor as I ran to the bathroom, praying that it wouldn't last long. I started ripping at the Pepto Bismol tablets in my pink flowered medicine bag. I sat on the toilet and thought, *Not today, please, not today.* I lay on the carpeted floor of the bathroom and the cramps kept coming. I jumped back on the toilet, then lay back on the floor, but the cramps were relentless. I could hear the girls stirring, and I told myself, *No, I can't miss this, I can't miss them running out to see if Santa came to Palm Springs. I can't miss Kierra seeing the doll that she so desperately wanted!*

But, of course, I did miss it. I could hear from the bathroom floor that my girls had woken up. I crawled along the rug on the floor to catch a glimpse of their smiles. But that was all I got to experience of their joy.

For the next twenty-four hours, I tried to figure out what was wrong with my stomach. Was it something I ate the day before? Was it the milk in the mashed potatoes? My family wasn't much help. My siblings took turns reminding me of the signs by the pool that said you couldn't swim for seven days if you had diarrhea. I survived the attack, but obviously didn't get to go swimming for the rest of the trip.

Back home, my doctor told me that I might be lactose intolerant, but that there was no good test for it. He said it would be best to try an elimination diet. After cutting out milk, I seemed better. Maybe it really was the milk! But then it would start up again. Sometimes the diarrhea was severe, sometimes it was just cramping. I went to the doctor again. This time he suggested that it might be diverticulitis. I went for tests, and nope, it didn't seem to be that. Then, I got better again. The severe pain came and went. Maybe it was a gallbladder attack, the doctor suggested. *Maybe,* I thought. I went for an ultrasound, and nope, no gall stones. *Maybe they passed? Or maybe it's just the lactose?*

***

During the second half of TMS treatment, my script focused on some of my biggest questions about people who can hurt others. I repeatedly ask the killers of Tori Stafford, *Why? How could you torture, rape, and kill an eight-year-old child? What could have been so bad in your childhood or with your brain that you felt it necessary to go after a little girl?* Another case that haunted me was Tessara and Samantha Crespi, two little girls whose father brutally stabbed and killed them one afternoon while playing hide and seek with them. How could a father do this to his children? How could two little girls deserve this ending?

Then I went even further – how could anyone justify the horrors that happened during slavery? How could someone rip children from mothers and sell them to someone else? How could men beat and rape slaves? How could someone take indigenous children from their homes, screaming for their parents, cut their hair and beat what they thought was the disgusting savage out of them? How could they force them to forget their own language, abuse them, rape them? All these victims were human beings, children. What happens to a brain that you can do such unspeakable things?

Then I started to think about Hitler and all those who brought him into power and supported him. How could you send people and children to die in gas chambers? And these horrible things continue into present day. How can Hamas have tortured so many innocent people, and the Israelis killed 25,000 people over the past four months. The victims are families just like us, who are ripped apart and murdered. How do people sleep at night with this on their conscience?

Then I turned to God, and questioned why he said, "Be not afraid" when there are so many things to be afraid of. I have always been afraid of death. I have these recurring thoughts that if there are billions in heaven and billions in hell, when does that end? It doesn't make sense that eternity is "forever" – forever surely must end. Then I sometimes look at it from the opposite side. When you die, you are just dead. How is that possible? How is a living, breathing, thinking, caring thing that laughs and has joy, has pain and tears, that questions God and eternity just stopped? Why is there life, and then nothing? How do I go from being the person writing these words to something that no longer exists? Now that scares the bejesus out of me, and is a much worse alternative than having eternal life and floating around endlessly.

It occurred to me that even though I am constantly plagued with these thoughts and violent images, I had not let on to the rest of the world that I suffered like this. People saw me as what I want them to see, and I was good at pretending. Even when I wanted to be authentic, I couldn't help but pretend. Friends had said to me:

Wow, you are so brave and courageous for wanting to live in Australia!

You have such beautiful skin.

You have the prettiest green eyes.

I love your thick curly hair.

You are so good at your job; we love working with you.

You are so fun to have at the party. Everyone loves having you around!

You are so positive, so kind, so caring, so emotionally intelligent about how others are feeling.

You are such a good mom; I would love to be your child and the birthday parties you throw are the best, and putting pumpkins on your heads was hilarious; your kids are living their best lives.

Your home is beautiful; your yard is gorgeous.
You are a great friend.
You have such great kids; they are so smart and well-mannered and kind to everyone at school.
I love that you take your family on vacations as a priority.
I love the scenic pictures you take.
You are so lucky; you have it all.

It felt like a sham. It wasn't that all those things weren't true, but they were only true on the outside. I had struggled my entire life to avoid the shame that comes with being different or mentally ill. The sham wasn't that it all happened, but that I made it all look easy. The sham was I was fighting a dark, dark illness and I never let anyone all the way in. The sham was that I never told my mom and dad, my brothers and sister, nothing.

Why the hiding? Why the masking? Why did I never want anyone to know how dark it was? I guess it was because I would have had to admit there was something wrong with me. But why would that be a stigma? You could easily tell if I had a broken leg, and no one around me would question that I'd broken my leg. Nor would they have thought I was any different, any less successful, or any less of a mother for having a broken leg. I felt like the stigma had changed since I was a child, but I was still compelled to pretend. I looked like I was a successful businesswoman, wife, mother, but I was a Barbie. I was plastic.

However, if I had told people all the things I had seen on a daily basis, well surely they would have helped me get help, but then I would have to be "that person."

Oh, did you hear? Michelle has gone nuts.
Such a shame. She seemed like such a good person.
I won't let my kids play over with hers.
Me neither.
Should we promote Bob to that new position, or should we promote Michelle?
Oh no, not Michelle. She has had all those problems.
I don't think she should drive.
I don't think she can look after her kids.
I don't think she is employable.

Oh, those poor Temple kids.

So, I wondered, had the stigma changed? Why was it okay to think *I'm a good mom if I have a broken leg, but not if I have depression*? Maybe it was just in my mind that the stigma hadn't changed, because that's the way I grew up. I knew that this next generation had a lot more in the way of mental health classes and working towards education about mental illnesses. I thought that was a good start. Just because we couldn't see the illnesses didn't mean that they didn't exist. A child must feel safe to be who they are, and feel what they feel, and know that the love of society is as unconditional as it would be if they broke their leg. I didn't know if other countries were ahead or behind us, but I knew there was still work to be done.

If I had known at nineteen years old that I could still be successful and fit into society, would I have said then that I had depression and violent thoughts of harm? Could that have changed the trajectory of pain my brain and body have suffered? If my mental illnesses had been regarded as a broken leg that needs physiotherapy, would that have been enough for me to be able to accept myself at that age? Could society's acceptance have saved some of the 700,000 lives last year who maybe like me couldn't live with society's perception of what illness looks like? Why would I hide that broken leg and let it get worse over the years when I could have got help and made it feel better? Society, my family, and my own expectations would have known that the broken leg didn't change anything else about me and I still could have been the world's idea of perfect. Why does mental illness have to be any different?

Maybe I'm just speaking from my own perspective, but it seems like the hope lies in the next generation, who will recognize their symptoms in themselves and others and seek help, instead of living with deep dark secrets and trying to keep their persona clean.

TMS Session Five

Today as the magnets hit my head, I found myself thinking again about the horrors people do to others. I began to see a connection between the horrific images I saw and all the questions I have and my own feelings about the innocence and preciousness of children.

Ever since my miscarriage, I had desperately wanted another baby. But I would often question if I was wise wanting to go through having a newborn again. Sometimes when I would wake up in the middle of the night to go to the bathroom, I would think, *You wouldn't want to get up like this every couple of hours now, would you? Remember how tired you were, how draining the constant needs were? You don't want to go through all that again, do you?* But my answer was always *yes!* No matter how much I yawned as I walked down the hallway, a little grin would form on my face, and I'd think, *Yes. I want to do it all again. I know there is a baby waiting for us and I just want to know who they are.*

Months turned into years, pregnancy tests became dreaded disappointments, and my optimism was starting to wane. I was thirty-nine and felt the possibility of becoming pregnant again was becoming slimmer and slimmer. It wasn't that I wanted to give up on another child, it was more like I thought I might have to let it go. My body was refusing to cooperate as easily as it had for the first three pregnancies.

One day I was at my breaking point, and decided it was time to stop trying. Really, I didn't think Kevin was that committed anyway, so I didn't think he'd mind.

"Kevin, I think it's time for us to give up trying to have another baby," I told him.

He seemed surprised. "But I thought you were really dedicated to the idea of a third child!" he said.

I was shocked. As I said, I didn't think he was really as into it as I was. "It isn't happening," I told him. "We've really tried, and I just don't think I am going to be able to get pregnant this time. Maybe we just aren't meant to have another child."

Surprisingly, he tried to rally my spirits. "If we can't have our own, there are still other options. We could look into adoption, even. Have you thought about that at all?"

I was shocked! "No, but that is a possibility. Let's give it a little while longer," I replied.

That was the spark I needed. I was going to be forty in ten months! It was now or never. Whether I got pregnant or I didn't, we had another choice – adoption! Somehow, feeling that safety net beneath me allowed me to relax, and I stopped stressing about it.

And wouldn't you know, on the morning of April Fool's Day, I sat there staring at a positive pregnancy test. *Really, God? April Fool's Day? This is how you are going to give this to me?* Apparently, it was. I took the test and ran full speed to Kevin, who I loved to trick every year on April Fool's Day. This was indeed the best one I could have come up with!

This pregnancy went fairly smoothly. I didn't gain a lot of weight; however, I probably started the pregnancy at 180 or 190 pounds. During this pregnancy I actually thought I looked nice with my cute pregnancy belly. The day of Brant's birth finally arrived, and we went to hospital, where he was delivered via C-section, like my other babies. We were thrilled to have a healthy baby boy!

***

In the second part of my treatment, where I had to read my script and envision the bad stuff, I found myself less and less worked up. The script almost looked like someone else had written it! It was terribly sad and awful, but I found I was not able to make it real in my mind. Every eight seconds as the magnet hit, I tried to bring up my awful visions, but my brain kept saying, "Nope. I don't believe that!" or "Nope, that doesn't sound right, that's not plausible, that's not who we are."

It was an internal tug of war, and I felt I was on the winning team this time! Maybe the magnets and all the work I had poured out was starting to disperse those cyclical thoughts to other logical parts of my brain. Cross my fingers!!

After returning home that day, I reflected on my life with Kevin. You see, I grew up on a farm, but I never ever wanted to be a farm wife. I wanted a city life, where we worked our jobs, shared responsibilities, had a modest mortgage, went camping in the summer and saved money for trips in the winter. Isn't it ironic that I married a farmer and moved back to my hometown. That's how fast these curve balls happen. Life is uncertain, for good or for bad.

But I did get to have my own adventure before we settled down on the farm. After I got my Chartered Accountant designation, Kevin agreed that we could get a home sitter for the farmhouse, rent out the land, and temporarily move to Australia. He knew I had always sought more than living on the farm, so he sacrificed a lot so that I could see the world and live by the ocean just once.

I don't think though that he regrets it one bit as it was a great time in our lives. I worked for Ernest and Young in Darwin at the time and we travelled everywhere for audits. We did lots of aboriginal reserves in the outback, and I even had to fly to a small island once to do another one there. We experienced new cultures and were immersed in the Aussie way of life. It was just the way I had imagined adult life would be: work during the day, have pool parties and fun at night, share responsibilities in the apartment, then take day trips on the weekend. We made lots of great friends in Darwin. Then Ernst and Young ended up getting a contract for the United Nations transitional government in East Timor as it rebounded from war with Indonesia. We got to be a part of that, and stayed in construction trailers with the UN army and even in a docked ship outside the headquarters. I met so many amazing people, wrote an internal audit manual for cash procedures for the UN and did amazing weekend trips. If we stayed two weeks in East Timor, our treat would be a weekend in Bali on the way home. Kevin started working for the railroad that they were building from Alice Springs, in the center of Australia, to the north port of Darwin, where we lived. He started making really good money at this job, and we were able to make more trips. Soon it was time to go back to Canada. I was excited to plan our trip home, spending three weeks in New Zealand and then one week in the Cook Islands. As it turned out, we flew across the international date line on our anniversary, and joked that we got to have a two-day celebration! Kevin gave me a gift of a beautiful necklace and earrings with an aqua stone. He told me the aqua stones were to remember our year and a half by the ocean.

Next thing I knew we were back home. Kevin was ready to start farming but had to try to build up some funds, so he worked in excavating, and I got a job as a finance officer at the Health Region. While it was a really good government job, it didn't thrill me or ignite any passion in me. There was a short stint where I got to come up with a business idea to get swaddle blankets made for babies, and that was fun. I also got to teach in seminars all the things I had learned from books like *The Happiest Baby on the Block*. I also had these hooded sleepers that Walmart was interested in marketing if I could get them made. I had some connections in Asia, and they made some prototypes. I started going to baby shows in neighboring cities and was starting to have good success in this area. My business name was, *Tips from the Mom Next Door* and news about me was starting to spread. I even had a news article posted about it.

But it just wasn't the right time in my life for this. My girls were little, and I was struggling through postpartum depression. I wanted to ignite my passion for work, but there was just too much going on. Kevin was trying to start the farm back up and we had many arguments. One day things got so heated that I smashed the mirror we had engraved for our wedding and punched holes in the drywall with it.

So, life took a different turn. I was approached by the accounting firm that I used to work for to be their chief operations officer and to manage their dual locations. I would oversee the partnership financial statements and payroll, do performance appraisals for all staff, oversee IT needs, hire, train, and fire staff. I also kept up with accounting and auditing standards and worked on new templates for our financial statements for our clients. It was a huge job and one that I enjoyed. My HR skills really grew during this time, and I realized that I enjoyed working with staff more than working with numbers. For the first time I was making over $100,000 salary, and was able to start putting some money away in RRSPs. I also put money into helping the farm grow.

Kevin's mom was our third at this time. When I had late meetings or Kevin was baling, she was taking the girls to dance or volunteering at preschool. She loved her "dollies" and welcomed all opportunities to be with them. But she started getting tired and weak in the spring when Kierra was seven and Ava was five. She had emphysema and COPD and eventually we learned she had interstitial lung disease which was very progressive.

She went on oxygen in very little time, and I went into full panic mode. I took time off work to take her to some appointments, and realized she could only walk a couple of steps at a time. I tried getting her to the right specialists as quickly as possible. Time was of the essence. I started to pick up things for home care, like bath chairs and a wheelchair, and every time I would start crying on my way home. I organized a home care nurse because she was having trouble staying alone at night – she would always be gasping for breath and needed her puffer or Ativan to calm down. She and I were very close, and I wasn't going to lose her. I was going full into getting a lung transplant or whatever she needed.

But her children recognized that she was not going to get better, and living the way she was living was hell for her. I selfishly didn't want to accept that. I wanted her sitting at the table on oxygen with a coffee in her hand because I needed her to be there. There was no part of me that wanted to let her go, and I refused to give in that she would be at peace if she were able to just pass on. When she finally did pass, I felt a hole in my heart, as by that point we had been close friends for almost 19 years. She was fifty-nine years old.

Kevin had been devastated watching her illness progress and then watching her die. I was not able to give him the time of grieving that he deserved. But I worked full time and tried to manage. There were girls to take to dance, work to do, and bales to be made.

By the following year we were at a crisis point. We could no longer do this without her help and things on the farm were falling behind. Kevin and I struggled, him grieving and me trying to make everything work while suffering with depression. Something had to give, and I ended up quitting my chief operations officer position to take a break and mentally re-focus and piece my family back together. I needed to get Kevin caught up on the farm, I needed to look after the girls, and I needed a mental break.

When I was at home during this time, Kevin was happy to have me out helping him haul bales, as it made him feel less alone, and the girls were happy to have Mom do their ponytails for dance. Even the dog was happy to have me home. The following year I took a job at Credit Union, where I was able to be a supervisor for four days a week. It was a huge pay cut, but I knew that I needed this for myself and for our family. This would be the year we had Brant, and my postpartum hit again.

Here is the "I feel sorry for myself" part of the story. I never felt sorry for the mental challenges I faced or the ongoing undiagnosed abdominal pain I suffered, but I did feel sorry for myself that life seemed so much harder than it would be if we had two paying jobs and shared responsibilities. After a hard week of work, where I had run kids to activities in neighboring cities, made every meal, and done piles and piles of laundry, I found myself sitting at the computer on a Saturday morning, bidding for some farm equipment. I was also making grill cheese for the girls, curling Kierra's hair, getting Ava's dance outfit tried on, breastfeeding Brant, all while keeping an eye on the auction on my laptop to make sure I bid at the right time. If I weren't feeling sorry for myself, I might be laughing at how ridiculous it was.

Don't get me wrong – Kevin was never lazy. He was a workaholic, and was usually outside from morning to nine p.m. spring, summer, fall or winter. Spring and summer were the worst, but none of the seasons were easy. There was fall work when he had to feed the cattle in the early morning and at night when the temperatures were really cold. There were vaccinating days where I prepared meals for crews. There were days we chased cows and I tried to breastfeed in the truck in between running in the snow. There were days where Kevin was upset and the cows ran by us.

In summer, I would go to the lake for two weeks and Kevin would try to get out there for a couple of nights. He tried to be there for all the big school events and for major moments. I arranged kids, made meals for company and cleaned the house, while he would just run in two minutes before they got there. I organized and packed everything for trips and even would load the suitcases in the car because he would come in two minutes before we were supposed to leave. He was working hard, and I was working hard, but to what end? What kind of prize do we get for this rat race? Do I get a piece of cheese at the end?

It was a very hard time. We argued a lot, and there were many times we resented each other. Neither of us were getting our needs met. We went to counselling and tried to dig into our issues, but everything seemed to blow up in our faces. We were almost at the end. He believed he was the work horse so that I could buy more things; I believed that if he was going to work like a maniac and we weren't going to be partners, I might as well get more things. We were unaligned.

Then there was Covid. That period gave us a lot more family time, because I worked from home. I don't know exactly what changed, but slowly, slowly, slowly, we were starting to see each other's side. We could go quadding after work, we could have campfires, I could go canoeing with the girls at the slough. The pace slowed down, and we were able to regroup, reset and refocus on each other.

During this time, I worked up from corporate accounting supervisor to corporate accounting manager, and became part of the senior leaders. I had a great boss, a corner office, I worked four days a week, and I was able to give my all to the job. At this point my mental health was stable and I was always able to focus on what needed to happen. I may have had moments in the evening quiet that the images would come haunting, but for the most part during the day I was focused and professional. I loved being involved in meetings, and was always engaged in finding solutions to any types of problems. I had a knack with people and without tooting my own horn here, I was quite a successful manager. I know this not because my boss said I was, but because my direct reports said I was.

Once my physical illnesses started to escalate, the mental health ones did as well. It became harder and harder to keep it all together, but what made a major difference at this time was that Kevin had become my great supporter, and I was his. We started to feel like a team, and we started to empathize with each other. This made all the difference.

TMS Session Six

On day six of TMS, I had a harder time focusing on the positives in the first part of treatment, and it seemed like most memories I turned to had some type of caveat tied to them. I thought about being a child, and tried to bring myself to good memories with my mom, like bike rides together and falling asleep in her bed. But my brain immediately shifted to the negative side of this story – her brother yelling at her, the fear she must have felt when he was mean to her. I saw myself as a child, being afraid for my mom when I would hear those stories. I knew that I always wanted to protect my mom and to take away her pain.

I remembered that recently my mom told me how strong I have always been. Looking back, I think that it came as a result of my wanting to protect her. When I saw her in pain, I knew I had to be strong. In fact, I protected both my parents by keeping from them anything that was going bad in my life. I always felt like I had to shield them from it – they had enough hurt, and I was strong enough to take it, so I went through my own difficulties on my own.

One thing I kept from them was my ongoing struggle with pain. The uncertainty about what was causing my abdominal issues continued for years, and I never went into it with my parents. One doctor thought that it might be endometriosis, which is a tricky disease to diagnose. According to the World Health Organization, endometriosis is "a disease in which tissue similar to the lining of the uterus grows outside the uterus. It can cause severe pain in the pelvis and make it harder to get pregnant." Endometriosis is not seen on ultrasound, nor is it found on a CT scan. It is only sometimes evident on an MRI. The only sure way to find endometriosis is to be opened up for surgery.

Eventually I did receive a positive diagnosis, and it came at a very strange time. When we found out I was pregnant with Brant, I knew that I was definitely finished with having children. However, I didn't want to give my gynecologist the go-ahead to tie my tubes until I was absolutely sure the baby was healthy. We decided to do the procedure once I delivered the baby, following the C-section.

So once Brant was here and wrapped up and laying on my chest, my doctor asked if I wanted to go ahead with tying my tubes. I confirmed it, so Kevin and Brant went off to recovery while I got prepped for the second part of the surgery. As I lay there on the table, trying to ignore what was happening beneath the tent that was draped over me, I heard my gynecologist saying something to the nurses.

"Where are your tubes?" he said.

The nurses didn't reply, and I realized the question had been directed at me.

"Pardon me?" I wasn't sure what was going on.

He sounded exasperated. "Where are your tubes?" he said again. "I can't find them."

I thought this was such a strange thing to ask someone in the middle of a procedure.

"I don't know! I have no idea!" was all I could say in response.

He elaborated by saying, "There is so much scar tissue I can't even find them." He kept digging around and finally said, "There! Well with all that endometriosis, they are so intertwined that you are lucky you had a baby. There was very slim chance that an egg could have gotten through there!"

What a relief – we had our baby, and I now knew the reason why it took so long for me to get pregnant. It was endometriosis! How it started or why, I don't know and likely never will.

The postpartum I experienced after Brant's birth was quite similar to the others except I felt a little more equipped and prepared for the emotional roller coaster ride of it all – the lows and highs, the anxieties and the intrusive thoughts. So again, I suffered with the terrible images in my thought patterns day and night. I saw my baby being smothered, choked, strangled with cords, and stabbed with knives. In response, I would imagine stabbing myself in the head until the images of the baby being killed were gone. Again, I went on Fluoxetine and it helped significantly, although I struggled with staying on it while breastfeeding. I was so worried about hurting the baby in some way down that I stopped breastfeeding, and it was awful. I cried and cried. I felt horrible about not being able to give my baby what he needed because there was something wrong with me and I needed medication.

***

During the second part of TMS, I continued to think about the constant pain I've put up with, and the depressing journey it's taken us to try to diagnose and treat it. Not only did I have endometriosis, as it turned out – I would later find out that I had a number of abdominal issues.

One episode in particular stood out to me. It started one morning when I woke up in terrible pain, like nothing I have ever experienced before. I had been in the bathroom, then had to lie down on the cold floor to try not to pass out. The pain was almost blinding, my surroundings were dark, and the cold floor soothed my head.

I heard my daughter Ava talking to someone from down the hall. "It's really serious this time," she was saying. "She isn't even talking,"

My silence was significant to them. I was always vocal – vocal about pain, vocal about joy, most of the time just plain vocal! I couldn't talk though, I couldn't moan, I felt I could barely breathe.

Thoughts raced through my head: *I've been here before, what did I eat? Was it the cream? Oh no I think there was maybe butter in that sauce?*

I still hadn't quite figured out if I was completely lactose intolerant, but something told me this was no ordinary lactose ache. I faded in and out, hearing the voices of Kevin and Ava discussing taking me to the hospital. Finally, Kevin helped me to the car. I remembered the leather seats squeaking under me as I got into the car. It was such a cold March night, and I felt the cold air blow through the pants of my cotton pajamas and hit my legs. As Kevin drove, I stared straight ahead and begged God to just make this stop. We got to the hospital, the emergency doors slid open, and I saw the familiar waiting room. *Please God, this time they must help me*, I thought.

We waited in my room for what felt like a lifetime, but was probably about a half an hour. A doctor came to the door and talked to us from there. He was wearing a mask that he held up with his hand. I couldn't even really tell what he looked like, and only saw his dark brown eyes peering at me from above the mask.

I looked at him and thought, *I know Covid is still a thing but really, all I have is abdominal pain. How contagious am I?*

I told him why I was there. He didn't even enter the room.

"I will give you some Toradol to help with pain," he said from the doorway. "If you start feeling less pain in a couple hours, you can go home."

I heard his words and my first thought was, *Yes! Please take this pain away! Give me everything you've got!*

Kevin heard his words and thought, *What, why? Why no testing, why no examination, why no discussion of history, why no bloodwork, why, why, why?*

A nurse came in, and Kevin said, "My wife is in so much pain and we don't know why. Isn't there any testing you can do?"

The nurse was empathetic, and agreed that more should be done. She went to speak again with the doctor.

"I'm sorry but he is busy. Hopefully this Toradol does the trick." She left us there and closed the door.

Eventually I felt better and was released. We figured it must have been a bad stomach bug. But of course, it wasn't that simple.

***

After the magnets stopped, I kept on thinking about my pain, and the long journey that is still not over to try to correctly diagnose and treat it. When I got home, I sat down and continued to trace that path of frustration, fear, and agony.

I remembered that a few months after the emergency room visit, where basically nothing at all had been done for me, I had another episode, this one finally leading to a diagnosis. My friend Angela, who had lost her young son the year before, had reached out to me about going to see our favorite musician, Bon Jovi in a video concert at a drive-in (due to covid). It was going to be over a long weekend in May, and she wanted us to meet up in Watrous. Of course I accepted! I was excited about seeing Angela, even though I was a little bit worried about what our conversations would look like. I didn't want to say anything wrong, but I wanted to support her in her loss and was happy to spend time with her and catch up. I bought her a crystal ornament with a dragonfly on it, as her son had loved dragonflies.

The day of the event looked like it was going to be another normal weekend day. Kevin was busy working with the calves that were coming and the seeding that needed to be done. I woke up and had coffee, but was too busy trying to get packed and ready to have any lunch. As I drove out of town, I decided to stop at McDonald's for a large coffee and some chicken nuggets. It was a three-hour drive to Watrous, and when I finally arrived it was about 5:00. Angela and I met at a restaurant, and proceeded to have vodka Caesars. I ordered some of my favorite dishes – lasagna and garlic toast – for dinner.

Afterwards we went to the drive in, parked, then went inside for some buttered popcorn and Coke. While I normally don't drink Coke, it's Angela's favorite drink, and they were serving them in old-fashioned glass bottles, so I joined her. We sat drinking the Coke and eating our popcorn and continued chatting. Finally, Bon Jovi came on, and as we watched from the car, I melted as I saw his smile. Now I am a happily married woman, but man he sends me into bliss just to see him perform. It was a wonderful show. We went back to the hotel and chatted some more, then went to bed. I was so happy I was spending some time with her.

But just like with a lot of my previous attacks, at 2:00 a.m. abdominal pain woke me up from my sleep. I tried not to move around too much or make any noise so as not to wake Angela. Holy cow, did it hurt though. I rolled over, changed positions, then finally made a mad dash for the bathroom. *Where is that pink flower bag of meds I always bring*? Too late! The diarrhea started just as I made it to the bathroom. I sat there in so much pain. I felt dizzy and weak. *Oh no! I'm going to throw up!* Thankfully, the diarrhea decided to subside for five minutes so I could throw up. Then I lay down on the cold, dirty, hotel bathroom floor. The linoleum was kind of a dark orange color, and the room reminded me of an old Alfred Hitchcock movie. We had used an actual key to get in!

I stayed in the bathroom all night, alternating throwing up and having diarrhea. I was in terrible pain. Then I saw that there was a lot of blood in my diarrhea. I knew something was very wrong. By then it was 8:00, so I woke up Angela and told her what was happening.

"This is similar to my other attacks, but I'm worried because there is blood in the stool," I said, hoarse from throwing up.

She responded, "You need to get to a hospital immediately. Do you want me to take you?"

"No, I can drive myself," I told her. "But I refuse to go to the one near my home. They have never been any help at all. They'll just give me Toradol and send me home."

Angela was adamant. "You need to go somewhere that will treat you. Do you think you can drive to Regina or Saskatoon, or is that too far? They can't be any worse than the one you normally go to."

I decided on heading for Regina, because then I could drive home from there. I hugged Angela goodbye, reassured her I would be okay, then climbed into my car. The cramps were like labor pains, coming every ten minutes. I don't know how I made it, but I pulled into Regina a couple of hours later. *I know this drill,* I thought. *They'll give me pain meds and send me home.* Then I got panicked, and began to pray. *Please God, if you're listening, please send me someone who will help me!*

And what do you know? It worked! In the hospital I saw a lovely female doctor, who actually listened to me and seemed to care. She was the kindest anyone has ever been to me in emergency. She told me that we were going to get to the bottom of it. She called the office of the doctor who she felt was the best gastroenterologist in the city. They decided I would have a colonoscopy the next morning. She advised me to go to a local hotel and do the preparation for the procedure, then show up back at the hospital at 8:00 the next morning.

Kevin offered to come and help me, but I really didn't want him to bother. From what I knew about colonoscopy prep, I figured I would be sitting in that hotel bathroom for the next four or five hours. After that, I just wanted peace and quiet and sleep. Kevin agreed, and said he would pick me up after the colonoscopy and drive me home. I left the hospital and the wonderful doctor, and went to a store to pick up all the items I needed: ginger ale, Jello, water and my prescription. When I got to the hotel, I started drinking the liquid for the prep. It went fine for a while, but of course, I ended up having a horrible experience. At one point I didn't make it to the bathroom in time, and had diarrhea while still wearing my pants. And I only had one pair of pants! I finally felt good enough to wash them out in the sink, then put them back on, soaking wet, and make my way back to the store to buy some new pants. But I finished the formula and was eventually able to rest for a while.

The next morning, I was back at the hospital. *Surely they will find something wrong with me!* I told myself. I went into the room for the procedure, met my doctor, and was soon pretty knocked out from the drugs they give you to make you oblivious to what they're doing during the colonoscopy. Suddenly I heard the doctors and the techs talking.

"I've never seen anything like this!" one doctor exclaimed.

"This is unbelievable!" said someone else.

Then I heard the main doctor say, "Get the interns in here; they need to see this!"

Oh great! As always, I was some kind of unique case!

As I woke up, the gastroenterologist told me, "Well, Michelle, for a forty-five-year-old, your insides look like those of an eighty-year-old!"

"What do you mean?" I asked him, almost afraid to hear the answer.

"Well, it appears that you have just had an ischemic colitis attack. We usually only see this type of attack in much older people who have cholesterol-filled arteries. You don't have that issue, so this is a complete enigma to us!"

"What does it mean?"

"You have ischemic colitis. It is extremely unusual in a person your age, as I said."

I had no idea what he was talking about. "What is ischemic colitis?"

"It's a condition where there is a blood flow blockage that causes the colon to shut off. From that point, your body decides it is time to evacuate everything up and down. It doesn't want any food in your system until the lining of your colon starts to heal. If you put food in, in a gentle way of speaking, your body will immediately and forcefully remove the food."

I was stunned. I had never heard of such a thing.

"Is there a cure? A treatment?" I asked.

"Well, I'm going to refer you back to your general practitioner for follow-up. Hopefully he can help you through a process of elimination to figure out what's causing it and get you a treatment."

Of course, that was easier said than done.

TMS Session Seven

In preparation for the seventh TMS treatment, I was told that I should say positive affirmations to myself: you are strong, you are brave, you are kind, you are thoughtful, that kind of thing. I told my tech last week that I didn't feel I was strong, brave, or courageous. I said I could say *kind* and *thoughtful*, but the rest didn't resonate with me. But during treatment, I kept going over the words, *you are strong*, and then it finally clicked in. I *was* strong! I got up every morning, made meals, looked after kids, made people laugh, did my job, looked after food, clothing, activities for the kids, helped them with their school needs, made appointments, chased cows, planned trips, packed for camping, went to events, volunteered, had lunch with friends, vacationed and walked trails, all when I was at my lowest. I felt that I didn't have a choice, but I did it anyway. I was strong! Everything looked perfect from the outside looking in because *I* made it that way.

I began to see my strengths, even if just a little bit. It was true that I refused to lie down on the floor and cry, because there was no way I was going to give up my children's childhood memories of a happy family. It was true that I refused to do a poor job at work, because deep down I knew that I was good at it. It was also true that I refused to sacrifice any moment of joy that I could get, even if it was just a few minutes of seeing the clear lake and the sunset. My mom said I was always strong, and I think as a young child I did feel if you wanted to enjoy your life, there was no other way to be. I never realized there was even an alternative until the magnets started to hit my head. I could have stayed in bed. I could have not worked. I could have let Kevin and the girls raise Brant. It was a choice that I made to do all those things and more. It finally clicked, and I can now proudly say *I am strong!* Now I don't mean to imply that taking a break when you need it is a bad thing, or something to be ashamed of. But accepting what must be done and realizing you are the only person who can do it is powerful.

Having said all that, though, the truth is that it's hard to carry on with your responsibilities. It's very hard. I wake up most mornings with weights behind my eyes. It's hard to describe them, but they are just what I would call the physical feeling of sadness. After six sessions of TMS, I am still having violent thoughts against myself. It's better, but not healed. Even last night and this morning, I would see a cord and want to wrap it around my neck. I would look at a knife and see it going up my nose and then plunging deep into my brain, so deep that there is nothing left for the brain to do but just give up and die. I walk around, make coffee, grab a glass of water, start making breakfast, and think about my day.

To all the people who struggle with illness or are just completely overwhelmed and tired, I see you. I think of you while the bacon is frying and while my eight-year-old flips the pancakes over the side of the pan and it drip-drip-drips on the counter. I feel bad for all of you who are doing the same thing. But for myself? All I can think is *Man, are you lazy! Wow, you are such a princess that you can't even make breakfast!* I wasn't born a princess, although sometimes that's how my parents treated me. Maybe when I have thoughts like these, it's just me reinforcing the self-image I've always had that I am so spoiled that I need someone else to take care of me. It perpetuates the self-hate and adds to my struggle.

I think about that whole "strong" thing again. Do I get up and make pancakes and bacon because I have a choice, or because I don't have a choice? I guess I have a choice. I could let the family find their own food in the fridge, but I would feel terrible if I did that. I know my mother had some hard times when we were children, and what did she do? She pushed on. She made my Barbie clothes on the sewing machine, she prepared homemade buns for when I walked in the door from school for lunch, and she always had dinner on the table for Dad and us kids. Even if I search and search my memory, there is not one day that she wasn't there.

Honestly if I asked her right now, in my depths of feeling sorry for myself, if I should take a break, she would say, "Lay down, honey. Let them handle this. They are adults."

"But Mom, that's not what you would have done. You would have fought through it. You never gave up!"

That's why I don't think that I deserve using the word *strong* to describe myself, because I just have to do it. I don't have a choice.

You know what saying I hate? *What doesn't kill you makes you stronger*. Why do we have to go to the depths of despair to prove that we are strong? You are strong just for waking up today. You are strong for making hard choices. You are strong for standing up to a doctor. You are strong when you plan to walk for five minutes and you end up doing 15 minutes. It isn't what almost killed you that made you stronger, it was you all along! It is in you to try and try harder, not just because you have to, but because that is just who you damn well are. It's been in there all along.

***

Although it was hard to switch from positive thoughts to triggers on day seven, during the second half of treatment I had planned to press myself to heal from the thoughts of little Tori Stafford. I saw the little girl screaming for her mother while she was raped and murdered. I thought about the woman who killed her with a hammer. My stomach still turned, and I still said *Why?*

While I pressed myself to heal from this, I thought of my theory of souls, and how we are each here for a different purpose. It came to me that I needed to leave their journey to them. It was not my soul's journey, and it was not my story to own or tell. I prayed that my logical thoughts would disburse this cyclical vision as I repeatedly told myself that was not my cross to bear.

As I continued to let my thoughts drift, I also connected that I didn't have any physical stomach pains until after my accidental baby miscarriage and D and C. I fully believed that the endometriosis didn't start until around eight months after that. I thought to myself, *All this time I could have avoided endometriosis if I had never lost that baby.* Life's uncertainties change you for better or for worse. If I had never gotten pregnant with my accidental baby and lost them, then I probably wouldn't have had the drive that I had to have my third baby. It kicked into gear that Brant needed to be on this earth but his soul wasn't ready yet. Brant would come when he was ready, not when I wanted him to come.

My homework was to write in a gratitude journal every night. I had a lot to put in it that day and it felt really good.

***

I still didn't know how the endometriosis was related to my later diagnoses. Maybe there was no relation, but I hadn't had a doctor confirm or deny that. However, I did eventually continue my journey to try to get answers about what the gastroenterologist had determined was ischemic colitis. It would prove to be a frustrating path.

A few days after my colonoscopy, I went to my doctor's office. He greeted me with a handshake, as always, and a grin.

"Michelle, with all my years of diagnosing patients, I would never have guessed you had ischemic colitis!" he exclaimed.

"Am I as unusual as that?" I ask him.

"Well, let's just say that no doctor, now or in the past, reading your case on a medical exam would ever, ever choose ischemic colitis for the answer!"

Well thanks, Doc! I think I've always been special to my parents, but I didn't know I had to be special at everything!

He outlines the plan of action. "First, we are going to see a blood flow specialist, then an autoimmune specialist, then we will continue from there."

"Do you think the endometriosis has anything to do with this?" I wonder out loud.

"To be honest, I really don't know. But we will try blood flow and autoimmune first, then see what that shows before we decide the next steps." That would be strike one.

So off I went on my trail of specialists to find out why I have this. The blood flow specialist walked into the room with a gruff, "I am better than you" attitude.

He introduced himself by saying, "I don't know what you are doing here. There is nothing wrong with your blood flow."

I looked at him speechless.

He continued. "I saw your blood tests. You don't have any cholesterol issues, so you, young lady, have been misdiagnosed." He looked up from the printout in his hands. "Only old people have ischemic colitis, and that is clearly not you. You can leave now."

Anger bubbled inside of me as I clutched onto my papers that I had printed out from the gastroenterologist showing that I had, in fact, had an ischemic colitis attack. While I am usually quiet and apologetic, with a "sorry for wasting your time" attitude, today I was not feeling it.

My voice rose as I spoke. "Really! Well, the best gastroenterologist in Regina says that I do, and if you don't believe him, then call him. Call him right now."

He was taken aback by my forcefulness I could tell.

"Okay, I will!" he grumbled, and left the room.

I sat there really pissed off. Ten minutes later he reappeared.

"Well, I was able to get ahold of your gastroenterologist, and it is a very rare finding, but you do indeed have ischemic colitis. I must admit, I have absolutely no idea why."

Strike two.

The next stop would be auto immune. I drove two hours to Regina for the appointment.

I was met with a very kind lady who told me, "I am really sorry, but I don't see any markers in your bloodwork for lupus, vasculitis or anything auto immune."

I could tell she saw from my face that I was crushed to hear this. "I feel terrible for you," she said. "If you like, I will put you on prednisone to reduce the inflammation. It may help the bowel attacks."

I knew she didn't really have any reason to do that except that she felt sorry for me.

"Thanks, but no thanks," I told her. "I don't need to go on something when there are no markers that I should be on it." Strike three.

Back home, I again spoke with my doctor about our next steps. We discussed the possibility of the endometriosis being linked to the ischemic colitis. He said that he didn't think so but that he was running out of theories and wanted to send me to a specialist in Regina. In the meantime, he said that if I had another attack, I should tell emergency that I had ischemic colitis, and that I would need morphine. He stressed that I would need to tell them to ensure that my bowels did not fully block or I could die. That felt pretty important, so I wrote it in my trusty blue folder, that I had started after my ischemic colitis diagnosis and was armed for my next attack.

TMS Session Eight

As I drove to treatment on day eight, I kept seeing myself being pushed under water. I would come up gasping for breath, then go down again, over and over until I was floating dead in the water. It did feel like I was drowning sometimes. I was tired that morning just like other mornings, tired of the magnets hitting my head while I struggled to grin and bear it.

In the first phase of the TMS treatment, when I was supposed to be thinking of positive things, I just couldn't do it. The magnet hit and my hand flinched hard. *Remember to breathe*, I reminded myself. It hit again; my hand twitched again. I tightened my grip around the pillow I was holding and settled into my breathing pattern, breathing in deeply, then out when the magnets hit. I tried to adjust my thoughts and get into a rhythm. I thought of something that brought me joy: the clear lake while I'm kayaking in the sunset. Within a second, I was pushed under the water and gasping for breath. I readjusted my thoughts, picturing my beautiful children who mean the world to me. I thought of their gorgeous faces, but suddenly I saw them as babies, being strangled and turning blue. I tried again: the smell of fire. I used to love it when Dad made a fire for me. But then intruding thoughts came. *Dad, I don't ever want to lose you. Please Dad, don't die!* I sat in silence, knowing that the second part of the treatment was going to be easy, since I was already in my dark place.

During part two, my usual script brought up all the vivid violent thoughts, but I had written a new script the day before, full of *why*'s. The tech had told me that sometimes when you are making progress, your mind fights back because it doesn't want to let it go. I pondered this as I read through the script.

"Why do you hate me so much? What have I ever done that is so bad that I deserve the punishment you bring? Why do you repeatedly show me images of harming myself or others to disgust and repulse me? Why won't you stop? "

I was met with the answer: *Because you don't want me to stop.*

"What? What did you say? That is preposterous! How dare you say that! You are a disease, and you keep trying to hurt me and I don't know why. Again, why do you hate me so much?"

I was told again: *Because I am you and you are me. I've been you all along. You throw hate at me all the time. You tell me all the time you are dumb, fat, ugly, and worthless. You tell me that you are not good enough. I'm showing you what I think you want to see, because that is what you believe. I think that you want and crave to torture yourself, so I give you the torture that you are asking for.*

"That's not true! I fight back! You started this with the awful images in university that I couldn't get rid of."

Wrong! You hated yourself first and this gave you an even bigger and better reason to hate yourself more. You had a terrible disgusting dark secret, and you wanted it that way. You wanted to take your hate for yourself and rub it in so deep that you couldn't escape. I help you to do that; you can't get rid of me because I'm driven by your own hatred.

"Nope that can't be true. I'm strong, funny, and successful."

True, but you don't believe it. Your hatred needs me like an addict needs cocaine. You can't like yourself now that I am here, but when you come close to trying to get rid of me, you fall back into your own hate.

"If the violent visions are not what causes my self hate, then what does?"

That's for you to figure out.

And the magnets stopped.

Wow. That was interesting. I was grateful that I brought all of that out of myself, but how to process it? I searched and searched my brain to find the triggers. I was aware of many of them – my weight, my self-image – but what was stuck in there so deep that it didn't want to budge? I had gone to a hypnotist years before to try to lose weight. Afterwards he'd told me that he had tried and tried to break my patterns, but there was something so deep that it was unbreakable to him.

I also thought the trauma of my ongoing pain and lack of treatment had contributed to my negative self image. Maybe that's because it was a part of me that I didn't want, a part of me that interfered with my life in a major way. I remembered one camping trip that was almost ruined because of what my body did to me. We had planned to meet up with family at the lake, and were leaving after my work. It was a Friday afternoon, and as I sat in my office, I couldn't wait for sun, sand, beers and conversation around the fire. However, my stomach had started making some awful rumbling sounds, and all of a sudden, I had to head to the washroom like my pants were on fire. As I sat on the toilet having the usual pains, suddenly the stall started to go blurry, and I thought, *Holy crap I'm going to faint in the work toilet with my pants down.* How's that for business casual? I tried to hold it together as the pain ramped up. Finally, I made it out of the bathroom and got back to my desk. I texted Kevin that I was going to try to get to the local emergency. I thought they would know what to do there, since I was armed with my blue folder full of instructions.

When I arrived, I was in serious pain and running back and forth to the bathroom. Waiting for triage, I went over the script that my doctor had told me to recite: *My name is Michelle Temple. I have ischemic colitis, I need morphine, and I need you to make sure that my bowels don't fully block.* When the nurse called me, I burst out my lines.

She looked at me with a frown and said, "The doctor here will decide what you have. You don't know what you have. And you will not be getting morphine."

Script fail. I was at the mercy of the attending physician. I'm so thankful, given my past experience with this hospital. I knew they would help me. NOT!

But when the doctor came in, to my surprise after doing the usual review of my chart and history, he said that he would call down a surgeon for a consult. In the meantime, I got Toradol, then lay down on the cold bed. Thankfully, my friend Shelly was on her way with socks and a sweatshirt because this was like a cold prison. My sweet niece had also met me in the waiting room to say that she really, really hoped I would get some answers so that I could get to the lake soon. Gosh, me too!

But when the surgeon arrived, he said that there was nothing he could really do.

"I can order you another colonoscopy," he said, "but that would take about a month or so. If it really is ischemic colitis, it will be long gone by then."

I sat and looked at him. "Is there nothing you can do for me now? I'm supposed to be going on vacation this afternoon," I pleaded with him.

"Well, what you need is to find out why you are having these attacks. Until you can find the cause, we can't really treat it."

Brilliant. Why didn't I think of that?

After I was discharged, I went home. Kevin and I decided to delay going to the lake by a couple of days. I was bummed, but in the end, we got there in time to enjoy several days with the family. However, once we arrived, I started to have a throbbing in my jaw. It got progressively worse, and soon I had to put the frozen Cool Whip container on it to get any relief. My niece who was studying to be a dentist was certain that I had an infection, and would need a root canal when I got home. She also said that I needed antibiotics. I desperately wanted to enjoy some time on the water, so I loaded up on Tramadol, gummies and alcohol to ease the pain, and headed for the beach. I'll be dammed if my stomach or my mouth was going to keep me from having a good time!

I got in the water and lay on the floatie, then I saw that my brother was giving rides on the tubes behind the boat. In my slightly drugged state I decided, *Sure! I'll go! There isn't anything wrong with me having some fun with the kids!* I was starting to feel loopy though, and as the tube got going, I started feeling like I couldn't keep my head up. So as we were riding along, I leaned back and put my head in the water, with my legs still crossed in this tube. Every bump shook my body in a really distorted way. I realized later that I was lucky I didn't get any back damage from that little adventure!

Then I was back on the floatie, sipping away my Black Fly, which is seven percent alcohol. I was getting increasingly more drunk, and by my third one I was singing out *7, 14, 21*, I was feeling good! No stomach pain, no tooth pain, just felt great. To be funny I decided to roll off the tube and stay under the water a little longer than I normally would, just to get the gang going. Of course, it isn't funny at all to pretend to drown, but in my state, I thought I was hilarious. Later as we were walking back to the truck, I started yelling out congratulations to Randy and Bev. I had no idea who they were, but someone had given me a cold sleeve from their wedding for my cooler. I started pretending that I was at their wedding. The kids and Kevin were laughing and shaking their heads. When we got back to the camper, I went inside and for some reason I climbed up on a step stool to reach up to get something. The stool slipped out from underneath me, and *bam!* I hit the hard flooring with a thud. I felt no pain, but began to laugh instead. I have no idea how many bruises I got that day, but damn it and all my illnesses, I did have a great time! I paid for it later with more nerve pain in my mouth, and I couldn't enjoy the afterparty. However, I did get to listen from my bed to the family banter coming from the campfire, and I was happy.

When we got home, I went back to my doctor to discuss endometriosis being the cause of these bowel attacks. I had been timing them, and it seemed like they came around the same time every two months. It was hard to tell exactly, since I no longer had periods, but it did seem tied in with my cycle. I was put on Lupron, a monthly injection that stops your body from producing estrogen. Kevin or my friend Shelly would pick a spot on my buttocks and insert a long needle, that to me was the size of a turkey baster.

Lupron made me feel like I wanted to die. I was so depressed, I had no energy, and I went to bed at eight p.m. because I wanted to hit my head into the wall. I was angry, mad, and annoyed. The kids at this time were 17, 15, and 6. At one point Kierra, the oldest, was starting to be fed up with having to do all the work in the house and feed everyone supper. She said I was being lazy. She said that if I ever did cook, I just made stuff that was unhealthy. When I heard that last bit, I was furious. I got up from the table, picked up my bowl and smashed it into the kitchen sink. Shards flew everywhere. I walked out the door, got in the car and started driving. I had no idea where I was going but I was seething with anger and had to get away.

I went to Dollarama and bought a notebook. In it, I wrote down all the meals I had made in the last month—homemade lemon chicken and rice soup, potato soup, chicken feta pasta, etc. I was going to show her! Instead, when I got home no one even seemed to care that I'd been gone for two hours. Life went on.

Later, I realized my daughter wasn't just being a brat. At the time I was thinking, *How dare she, with all I have done for her? I've worked so hard, providing her with everything she needs!* But as it turned out, she was scared, sad, and upset that I was no longer the mother she had come to know. It was the boldfaced truth staring at me. She was totally right. I didn't feel like myself, I hated myself, I was so depressed, I hated everything about being on Lupron. However, my physical attacks were lessening, so the doctor decided to rush me in as quickly as he could to remove the endometriosis around my bowel, ovary, and uterus. I was relieved; if I could get off the Lupron, maybe I would feel more like myself.

TMS Session Nine

When I arrived for the ninth day of treatment, I focused my positive thoughts on how I tried to find hope where I could. I wondered a lot about what we were all here for. Why were all these little minions frantically racing off going to work, to travel, to camp, all just to entertain ourselves? Yes, we had to make money to live, but I felt like society was just something we had randomly created, and purchasing things was just a way to spend our time. We didn't do all this work for food and shelter, at least most people in this country didn't. We did it for boats, cars, fancy houses, to travel, to watch sports – it was all just entertainment for us humans until we died. If God did exist (which I believed he did, by the way,) what was he doing this for? And if he didn't, then why was this planet randomly floating through space, with all these people on it running in all directions, lined up with their cars to get to their offices or their cottage at the lake or their parents' houses for holiday. And then they died.

Kevin sometimes would tell me that it was the amazing moments that make it all worth it. So I thought of a baby's giggle, a kiss on the cheek, the smell of the rain, the ocean breeze, the glorious sunset, a hug, a laugh – we were here for all these moments. We were here to help each other. I thought that for every connection we made, and for every terrible awful thing that happened to us, that we were here to help others. We were here to make them smile, give them hugs, friendship, and love. I thought that maybe when really crappy things happen to us, it was because it gave us a chance to give something to someone else. It was like the burnt toast theory: imagine you're making toast and it burns. In the time it took you to make new toast, you were saved from something worse that could have happened in that time. Maybe my toast had burned because it was meant to show hope to someone else who was struggling. If that was what I got out of these burnt toast illnesses, well then, I guess the least I could do was use my time to help others who didn't see the hope in trying.

***

During the second half of treatment, I thought about the combination of mental and physical pains I have worked so hard to resolve. Not having any answers had really affected me. The physical pain had started to make me feel hopeless. I would spend hours on the bathroom floor with deadly cramping, and at points, I would visualize smashing my head into a wall, or cutting out my stomach.

There were so many times I thought my family would be better off without me. *Who needs a mother who's constantly on the bathroom floor crying?* If I wasn't there, they could enjoy their life so much more. I was a burden. Because of me, the girls had to do so many chores to help on the farm. They couldn't go anywhere with me anymore because every time we tried, we would have to leave early, with me in agony and crying in pain all the way home. I was ruining their fun. I was ruining my fun. I felt so done with it all. I had started to feel that if I kept on like this, pretty soon I wouldn't have the strength to pull myself off the floor. I loved to be social and I loved to have fun. This wasn't living for me.

Eventually I talked to my doctor, telling him that my depression was unmanageable, and that it was severely affecting me and my family. He was concerned enough to push up my surgery date, thinking as I did that if we could stop the endometriosis from growing, I would feel better mentally and physically.

I was relieved. *I can't wait. Let's get this over with and get on with my life,* I thought. I was a bundle of nerves leading up to the surgery. Kevin and I got a hotel room, as we had to be up very early that morning. He was supportive and calm, and I was thankful for that. I snapped a selfie of myself at 7:00 a.m. and sent it to my mom, saying *I am ready!* I got my surgical gown on, put my hair in a hair net, and the nurses started prepping me. But one hour before I was supposed to go in, I received a visit from my doctor.

"I'm really sorry, Michelle. I have some unfortunate news," he said gently. "My co-surgeon was diagnosed early this morning with Covid. I've been looking for a replacement, but I don't want to take just anyone."

Oh no!

"Given the complexity of the surgery – any wrong move could nick your bowel – I didn't want to risk using some random surgeon."

Well, no! I didn't want just anyone off the street cutting around my organs! Of course I was disappointed, but I went home and waited for his phone call. Thankfully, it came only three weeks later. However, this time, Kevin had been exposed to Covid! He was also in the middle of baling. If you don't know much about farming, that meant he couldn't be my support guy. There was hay in the field that would be ruined if it wasn't baled in time, which would mean a huge loss for the farm.

So Mom and Dad quickly said they would go with me. I love my parents, but with Dad being eighty-nine and Mom seventy-six, I wasn't sure that they could maneuver me around after the surgery or get all my medications and items I would need in the city. I happened to tell my sister-in-law that they were taking me, and she quickly said that she and my brother would drive the two and a half hours and book a hotel next to us in order to help out. I was so grateful. With this plan, Mom and Dad could look after me, and she and my brother could essentially look after my parents and take care of any running around the city that needed to be done.

Everything went well the morning of the surgery. My dad even sat by my bedside while I got my IV started. He quietly told the nurse that never in his eighty-nine years had he ever had an IV or stayed the night at a hospital. She chuckled and I smiled – I couldn't imagine!

The procedure would be laparoscopic surgery, and I had decided to have them take my uterus and my remaining ovary as well as treating the endometriosis. This made the surgery slightly more complicated, since they would have to also remove the cervix and sew a vaginal cuff.

The surgery went well, but recovery was hard.

I had only been in the recovery room for about an hour, when a nurse woke me up and said, "Come on, Michelle. You have to get up and try to walk around some. Wake up!"

I could hardly talk. "I'm so incredibly tired," I told her. "It's like the kind of tired you are when you are little and your mom and dad are carrying you into the house."

"But you have to start moving around," she said. "I know it's hard."

"Can you please let me sleep just a little longer?"

She shook her head. "I can't. We have to have everyone cleared out by 2:00 p.m."

So my surgery had ended at noon, they let me sleep an hour, and I had to be picked up by 2:00 p.m. *Wow*, I thought, *what a wonderful medical system.* NOT!

"I will get you some ice pops," she said, "and maybe that will start to wake you up."

She finally got me up walking. I went to the bathroom and got my things together, then got dressed. I was still very groggy when the family came and got me, but I was thankful I could now put this whole mess behind me.

The next week I stayed at my parents for several nights. It was so quiet there compared to our bustling farmhouse that I soaked it up. I napped a lot and took short walks, and my mom catered to my every need. Yes, I was forty-seven, but I was still their baby and was definitely treated as one. I decided to go home when I was started to become mobile.

I felt fairly good at home until one day about a week after the surgery. My parents came out to dig potatoes from my garden and I needed to find the pitchfork for Dad. Thinking it wasn't very heavy, I carried it back from the barn. But for some reason I was struggling, and my body was shaking. I thought I must have just done too much. The next morning, I woke up with a fever and I was in severe pain. I was crying, agitated, emotional and just felt so, so sick. Usually, I try to not worry my parents, so I keep it to myself when I'm not feeling well. However, this time, I called my mom in tears. She suggested Ava drive me to the hospital because Kevin – you guessed it – was out baling.

So my fifteen-year-old child Ava drove me to the emergency room. I tried to be strong for her, but cried the entire way to the hospital. The medical staff was a lot swifter this time, knowing that I'd had surgery the previous week. When my blood tests came back, it was clear that I had an infection. I went for a CT scan, and the result showed that I had a pelvic abscess about the size of an orange where they had sewed me up on the inside. They were going to start two strong antibiotics via IV, but I would have to go home afterwards because there weren't any beds in the hospital. After that, I would have to return to emergency every eight hours for the next four days.

Kevin arrived around midnight. He was shocked that they expected us to drive back and forth for IVs.

"Can you not find some way to keep her here?" he asked. "She's still so sick that I don't think it's good to have her do that much travelling between home and the hospital. It's an hour round trip."

The nurse told us, "We can't do that. It's against the instructions we were given. I can allow her to stay until 8:00 a.m. But you'll have to leave then."

Kevin and I agreed, since it was better than nothing.

"But how are we supposed to transport her back and forth, feeling as bad as she does?" he asked.

"I can't help you with that," the nurse said. "Perhaps if you call home care, they can do something."

Eventually they gave me my first two doses of the antibiotics, and we went home. We called home care, but they said that since it was a long weekend, the best they could do was to have us return to the hospital that afternoon, and they could give us the IV and the supplies and teach us how to do it at home.

Once again, Ava drove me to the emergency room. She took on the task of learning how to do the IV. One of the medicines hurt as it went in, but the other one was painless. Back at home she woke me up every eight hours over the next four days. Some days she had to get up at 4:00 a.m. and warm the cold antibiotic for half an hour before she woke me. Then we discovered that if we heated a flax bag and put it on my veins, it didn't hurt as bad. Ava was so much help to me, but one day she was so sick of me watching *Virgin River* on TV that she begged me to watch anything else! But I found that somehow the show gave me so much comfort.

During this time, I was taking estrogen as a cream on my arms, and my depression and sadness had become overwhelming. I felt like crying every day. I had no energy, and I felt like I had a heavy weight on my eyes. I phoned my surgeon, who decided to put me on a birth control pill. He thought that maybe I needed more estrogen than what the cream was giving me, especially because I was on the younger side to have no ovaries. About a week after that, my bowel attacks came back. The first one happened as I was driving to the field to take supper to Kevin. When it struck, I had nowhere to go but out in the field. Thankfully, we had disposable masks in the car – I knew those things were good for something! I prayed I was just sick with a stomach bug or had eaten something bad.

    I had promised Kierra a five-day road trip to Montana for her graduation, and against the wishes of pretty much everyone, I decided to go ahead with it. I felt like my illness had already taken so much away from my children, and I didn't want it to take this trip from Kierra. We would be staying five to six hours from the border of Alberta or Saskatchewan, and if I got sick, Kevin was going to hightail it back to Canada. Yep, it was risky, but I wasn't having much fun these days, so this was my rebellion.

    The trip was awesome, but one night close to the end of the trip I overdid it. We had gone to a rodeo, where I had a couple of alcoholic beverages and some greasy barbecued pork from one of the vendors. The sky that night was a glorious red against the mountain backdrop as the star-spangled banner was sung and the horses came out running. It was immersion into the Montana culture at its finest, and I loved every minute of it. When we went to bed that night in our Airbnb, and it was probably only an hour until I started to feel the cramps that I knew so well. I ran to the bathroom. I was also vomiting this time. It was super tough to lay on the bathroom floor and curl into my well-known ball and endure the diarrhea cramps when I was jumping up every two minutes to vomit or use the toilet. The night was endless, and by morning, Kevin had come to the bathroom and asked if he should start driving to Canada. I said it was time to go home anyway, and that I would dose myself with Gravol and painkillers so that I could sit quietly in the car while they did one more round of horseback riding in the mountains.

    We made it back home, but the following week it came again, and then again. My surgeon had no answers, but said he was going to get me to my gastroenterologist as quickly as possible. He said he had nowhere else he could think of for me to go. I was completely distraught, knowing that this was the same gastroenterologist who just a year prior had said he couldn't help me, and that I "needed to find out why I was getting these attacks." Why could no one give me an answer?

After a straight month of weekly attacks, I felt I had nothing left to give and nothing left to throw up. I had gone to the emergency room as well during this time, and I was again and again given Toradol and told that there were no beds for me. I didn't know what to do. The feelings of depression were horrible as well, and I prayed to see a light at the end of the tunnel. Thankfully, my sister-in-law Tammy convinced me I needed to check out the Mayo Clinic in Phoenix, Arizona, they had a house in Palm Springs so we could possibly arrange for them to be with me there. I was fearful even mentioning this to Kevin as I had no idea how much it would cost. He was apprehensive but it wasn't an all-out no.

We talked to my general practitioner about next steps, and he said we could look for other specialists in the country but that with the pandemic, some places had not recovered back to full service. He said they would put me on the waitlist, but that it could take a year or two to get answers. Oddly enough, he also suggested the Mayo Clinic, and said if we did that, he would follow any medical plan they laid out. That way we could do any follow up in Canada to save money. It was a really big decision and a really big step, but I didn't want to go on like this, and my repeated thoughts of smashing my head into a wall or putting a bullet in my brain weren't helping. I told Kevin that I had to do something, and I was out of options. I couldn't believe it had come to this.

TMS Session Ten

It was my tenth day of TMS, and I got my first assessment. My psychiatrist told me he didn't want me to work during the full-time treatment period of eight weeks. I looked at his paperwork, and read the words *Diagnosis: Major Depressive Disorder and OCD*.

"Is this me?" I thought. How on earth did I get here? I was a successful mother, farm wife and manager…surely, he must be talking about someone else.

I'd heard that when you are sick, it is not the sickness making you tired and making your muscles sore – it's your immune system making sure you stay in bed and get the rest you need. Could it be the same for depression? Had my brain been forced to send me bigger and bigger signals because I hadn't listened or taken care of it?

During treatment, I reflected on how all my life, I had pushed down my depression symptoms, packed them up and put them in a box. I'd locked the box and thrown away the key. The thing was, they never truly went away. They might have been hidden away temporarily, but when the stress levels continued to rise, something would eventually come out. I thought about the self-hate and the way I have tortured myself with violent obsessive thoughts of harm. Were those thoughts my brain's way of making me tired, so I would rest? Was the self-hatred a way to finally make me see that I needed to do something? Your body could only give you so many hints, after all.

This thought made me realize another symptom that I have been ignoring and pushing down. It felt like it was related to my depression and my habit of ignoring warning signs. I had a problem with clutter. My house was full of it – in the basement, in the storage room, in the kitchen – it never ended! Every once in a while I would try to clean out the storage room but it was overwhelming. For years I had just thrown stuff in there and tried to ignore it, even though things fell off the shelves and on top of me when I tried to go in there. It was full of old satellite cables, party decorations, half-used hard playdough, a few plastic figurine Smurfs that I had as a kid…I had tried to start organizing it, then ended up piling it all in a box to throw away. Well, everything but the Smurfs, of course. Then I just sat there staring at it. There was even a glass jar of tomatoes in there, which I was sure would probably fall on my head next time I opened the door. Then I would have a big mess to clean up.

Kevin always said that with farming if you neglect anything, even something that seems small, like a fence missing one of its wires, without a doubt, that would be the spot where all the cows would break out. What might have been a half-hour job will turn into a six-hour mess. The key was that you couldn't fall behind. But somehow, I couldn't manage to keep up with it all.

I couldn't help but think of that storage room as my brain. It was so cluttered, but there were things in there that were valuable to me, mixed in with the garbage. Instead of preserving the things that I found valuable and useful, I wrote off the whole room as messy, disgusting, jumbled. It was so much easier to shut the door and ignore it, just like shutting off a part of yourself that you couldn't stand to look at. Or you might use some kind of band aid solution, like cleaning up the front and knowing that the back was still just full of shit. If you could numb the pain with the band aid solutions, or the complete denial of it all, it didn't exist. Why should my brain be any different than my house?

Here's the thing though – one day that glass jar of tomatoes would fall, smash into a million pieces, and scatter tomatoes everywhere, and you would have to clean it up. If you didn't, the food would rot, it would start to stink, and eventually you would no longer be able to live there.

Was your brain the same? As long as the pieces all held together for the moment, we kept on going. We might use alcohol or drugs to hide what's shoved back in there, or we might just deny it was there. But it came out in other ways. For me, it came out when I saw myself slitting my wrists every time I closed my eyes and lay down to rest.

So without numbing the pain or being in denial, was it possible to look at what was really in your brain? Who are you? Could you visit past hurts and make peace with them? Could you take those events and keep what was good about them and throw out the pieces that no longer served you? Admitting who I am and what my brain has done all these years was like staring at a warehouse full of clutter. How would I clean this and make something meaningful out of it?

One day the pieces would fall if you didn't take the time to organize what was on the shelf. My pieces fell; the tomatoes smashed to the floor. My brain couldn't hold its contents anymore. It needed to be taken care of and it needed to be put in order. It was time to throw out the garbage and keep what was valuable.

I saw that I needed to do this one old cherry pie filling and one hot sauce bottle at a time. If not, I would have more than a smashed glass jar of tomatoes. If I continued to ignore the clutter, I would further hurt myself and the family and friends who love me and want to be with me. It could take us years or decades to clean up the mess. But every day that I do TMS, more of the garbage will get thrown in the dump, because my brain will start to realize it's garbage.

***

Following consultation with my doctor and planning with Kevin, we did end up going to the Mayo Clinic to try to find answers to my bowel attacks. There I was met with the kindest hearts and a place that was like a movie to me. The cafeteria served Starbucks coffee and was upbeat with tunes of Pink playing in the background. Line ups for appointments were always less than five minutes, and everything ran like a well-oiled machine. It was such a refreshing change from what I had experienced at home! The doctors were sincere and empathetic, and not once was I told "if" or "maybe" or "we'll see." Instead, they said, "We will find the answers," "We will get you better," and "We will get to the bottom of this."

I went through a lot of tests: MRI, CT, colonoscopy, endoscopy, lactose test, and much blood work. The pelvic MRI included putting dye into my bloodstream. I didn't realize until afterwards that I might have a reaction to it. After the procedure I started throwing up, and I messaged my doctor (yes it was that easy, I just messaged her… I was blown away by this!) She said that in a small fraction of people, this can happen. She said that she was extremely sorry, but endometriosis patients are the main ones usually affected in this way. Her apology meant so much to me. She was genuine and authentic and was actively trying to help me. She had made a mistake and apologized for it.

That night Kevin took me to a fancier restaurant, because for the next test I had to eat straight chicken breast with no oil or seasonings. The only place he found to do that was an expensive high-end Asian restaurant. But sadly, it wasn't long before I had to excuse myself and run outside. I started throwing up by our rental car outside the window of all the high-end diners. I'm sure that restaurant was so glad we picked their establishment for dinner that night. Kevin took me back to the hotel where I continued to throw up until nothing was left but bile. I found myself laying on the cold bathroom floor. This time, at least, I had a reason.

Kevin was with me for the first few days and my brother Kelly and sister-in-law Tammy took care of me for the rest of my trip. Their support went above and beyond, and I can't tell you how grateful I am for them on this journey.

Within a day, my doctor had messaged me the results of the MRI. She said that she was concerned about a few things. One was that there was scar tissue that must have encircled the pelvic abscess infection I had after the laparoscopic surgery I had. The scar tissue had fused together my bowel, bladder, and vaginal cuff. This could eventually become further entangled and might require surgery. The second concern was that there was active new endometriosis growing on the end of the vaginal cuff. She said that as strange as it seemed, the endometriosis might be creating its own estrogen. If that was the case, it could use the estrogen to fuel its own growth. So even though I had my ovaries and uterus removed to stop the estrogen cycle, the disease might be able to continue to feed its own growth! It was concerning to have seen it grow within a couple of months, since the surgeon had cut out all the rest of it.

On the other hand, my CT was normal, as well as the colonoscopy and endoscopy. There were no present signs of ischemic colitis, which made sense, as I hadn't had an attack in almost a month, so my colon would have been healed. The lactose test after all these years was negative.

The doctor and I were able to put the puzzle pieces together and deduce that the bowel attacks came when 1. my estrogen was high, 2. I was dehydrated, 3. I had eaten something greasy, 4. I had a partial constipation blockage, 5. I had little activity or exercise, or 6. I was experiencing stress.

She also said that ischemic colitis was not only for old people; she saw it very frequently in runners. She said that when they get dehydrated, their veins become thin, causing a blockage in the bowel, which has the tiniest veins. Add a little clotting from estrogen to the equation, and it was a mic drop!

She passed me on to an endometriosis and a menopause specialist. Both agreed that I should go off the pill for estrogen, as it was a probable contributor to the attacks. The menopause specialist put me on a different drug for depression, Pristiq. It would also help with the hot flashes. I was also put on a low dose estrogen patch. Estrogen to me seemed to be a key driver in my mental health, but I was caught in a crossfire: I needed it to combat my depression, but having less of it really helped my physical issues.

The menopause specialist also ordered a gene test to find out what antidepressants worked the best for my liver's metabolic rate based on my personal genetics. They used these in pharmacies at the Mayo Clinic, so they could ensure that the person was getting the best drug with the most efficacy and least side effects for their personal genetics. Wow, now that was amazing! There were a few things were revealed by that test to help with future meds I was prescribed, but the most important finding to me was that I had the COMT gene variation AA.

The COMT gene is responsible for producing an enzyme called catechol-O-methyltransferase. Catecholamines include dopamine, epinephrine, and norepinephrine. They are produced in response to stress, and they are responsible for increasing heart rate, blood pressure, breathing rate, muscle strength and alertness. They also play a role in increasing blood flow to major organs like the brain, heart, and kidneys. COMT is one of the enzymes involved in the breakdown of dopamine in the brain. Common symptoms of mutation include estrogen and dopamine imbalance and poor detoxification.

In an AA variation, the person:
-is more creative
-has higher IQ

- has better motor skills
- has better verbal memory and reading comprehension
- has a more positive outlook towards life

An AA variation is also associated with:
- addiction and mental disorders, like ADHD, OCD, and Schizophrenia
- a lower pain threshold
- more sensitivity to stress

I was amazed to have received such a detailed and useful diagnosis. The Mayo Clinic was a dream come true. However, when I got home it was back to reality. Every doctor or pharmacist I talked to about this in Saskatchewan had nothing to say about it. While they were clueless, I was still relieved, because it provided me with some clarity about my genetic makeup.

So I went home with a lot of answers and a lot of plans to look after myself properly to avoid bowel attacks in the future. Hopefully, the low dose estrogen patch and the Pristiq would also help the depression.

TMS Session Eleven

On the eleventh morning of TMS, I woke up sad – sad that I had to go for treatment, sad that my violent thoughts weren't stopping, sad and worn down and tired. I was supposed to focus on positive thoughts as the magnet tapped above my eye and my body flinched. I was searching. I was searching for happy thoughts. My tech said to repeat my affirmations: *I am strong, I am brave, I am capable.*

As I was doing that, I began to visualize two wooden boats sitting by a dock, with some people in each of them. I could hear them talking…one of them was saying that the water was extremely rough, but if we wanted to get to the other side we had to try. I quickly got into one of the boats. I didn't know what was on the other side, but I knew I had to go. As we started to row away and I saw the big waves, I looked back at the rest of the people who stayed on the shore. I realized that I would always be the person who faced the rough sea, taking a chance to go forward rather than staying where it's safe. I was courageous. I would rather die trying to get somewhere than staying behind and wondering, *What if?*

During my back-to-back treatments of TMS today, I cried the entire time. Not from the physical pain but from the weight of constantly fighting my brain. The tech told me that she saw this a lot. As soon as you make a lot of progress, your OCD and anxiety start to fight you harder – they fight back because they want to win. All I knew was that I was angry, sad, and tired of it. I was also tired of expectations, maybe everyone's or maybe just my own.

I was having trouble understanding how I could have such an evil person inside me, one who kept showing me images of hurting myself. I honestly didn't want to die. I had always thought that if I had cancer, I would fight to the bitter end to make sure I was here for my kids and family. But somehow this disease did the opposite. Not only did it make me not want to live, it put little movies in my head of my own death that played throughout the day. I watched myself slitting my wrists, putting a gun in my mouth, even making sure that I fired it upwards so it could blast through my brain and end it all. One afternoon I had gone for a walk so I could put some things away in a grain bin that we had converted into storage. This made me remember someone I knew who had hung himself in a bin. This one was made differently, though, so as I put my stuff down, I looked around it to see where you would hang the rope. I couldn't find any good spot, but still I envisioned myself hanging there. Then I looked some more. *I think this may be a good spot,* my brain said. I said, *Shut up, brain. That is not what I was thinking, and it's not what I want to do.* It kept pressing me though, and I started falling back into a cycle of frustration.

I felt like a lot of this might be related to the COMT AA variation that the Mayo Clinic found during my genetic testing. My psychiatrist believed that my OCD was my primary condition and depression was secondary, a result of the OCD. But I was starting to think that most likely the self-hatred came first.

***

After my trip to the Mayo Clinic, I had coasted along for a bit. But I began to feel like I was suffering from CPTSD thinking about my symptoms starting up again. I was so scared of every little pang of pain, fearing and not knowing if it would turn into a major attack of pain and cramping. But despite that, my mood seemed fairly stable as I was happy to have some answers regarding my physical issues.

But then things started to go off the rails. I began to see images again – horrific, violent images. I would imagine my son, who was now seven but still a baby in my mind, lying in a ditch with his face buried in water, and when I would run up to him and pull him out, he would be dead and blue. I started to notice ropes and knives again, and the old images came flooding back in a rush. I would see my own children and strangers in horrible violent situations. Sometimes it would happen every hour and sometimes every five minutes. I would see myself stabbing my stomach, legs, head, and gouging my eyes out. The images were insistent and gripping and scary!

I went to my general doctor, who suggested we try an anti-psychotic to go along with the Pristiq. I messaged the Mayo Clinic and the menopause specialist agreed, and wanted me to go on Risperidone. I had just lost weight because of my physical illness, and I desperately wanted to stay that size! I knew one side effect would be weight gain. However, Kevin repeatedly told me that me being happy was better for everyone, including him. So I began taking it, and started going to therapy again. But I started sliding downhill into the darkness of depression, which I knew so well. I finally asked my doctor for a psychiatric consult; in all my life and all I had been through, I had never actually had a psychiatrist assess me.

I told the psychiatrist all about the thoughts and my history, and I didn't hold anything back. Within the hour, he told me that I was one of his rarer cases. He said what I was experiencing was called Harm OCD.

He explained it to me. "Harm OCD is when you have violent obsessions, with the compulsion being thoughts of hurting yourself to stop the obsession. It is similar to a person who obsesses over germs and has to wash their hands to try to stop the obsessive thought. This then becomes a cycle that doesn't stop. It's completely intrusive and debilitating."

It made so much sense, and perfectly described what I was experiencing.

He continued, "I have only had one other patient with this condition. I hate to say it, but I find schizophrenia easier to treat than OCD, because there isn't a medication specifically made to treat it."

"Can you give me anything for it? I can't continue the way I've been going," I told him. I was hanging on by a thread.

"What I would like to do is try to get a good combination of an SSRI like Fluoxetine as first defense, and an anti-psychotic like Risperidone as second defense.

His first step was to cut out the Pristiq and ramp up the Fluoxetine within a matter of weeks. It was disastrous.

My thoughts were overwhelming; the depression was overwhelming. I couldn't stand living with those thoughts all the time. It was constant – when I was driving, when I was cooking, when I was trying to enjoy my children. The only time I escaped it was when I slept. And so I slept a lot, mostly because it quieted my mind when I couldn't listen to it any longer. Mentally I felt worse than I had ever felt in my life during this medication transition.

One day, I got a gift at work that had a macrame plant hanger in it. I picked up the plant hanger, and what I experienced in that moment wasn't a thought – it was the strangest reality I'd ever felt. As I picked up the macrame rope, the touch of it told me that it was perfect for hanging myself with. It was so powerful. I had never experienced a touch that didn't even start a thought, but led directly to a conclusion, which was to hang myself with it. I managed to shake off the feeling eventually, but it was hard.

Then came a regular day just like any other. I was going to work and dropping Brant off at summer camp. Something was different though – I felt different. I put Brant in the car and started driving, but it felt like my mind was elsewhere. I had other plans that even I wasn't completely aware of. I knew I was dropping Brant off at day camp close to my office in the city, but the thought hit me that I could work from home. If I didn't show up at work, they would assume I was working from home. Kevin wouldn't know if I didn't go to work, because he had no reason to think I would be anywhere else.

All of a sudden, I felt that after I dropped Brant off at camp, that would be it. I was done. After I left him and said goodbye, I got back in the car and pondered what I was doing exactly. I found myself a block away from the hospital, but I knew they were not going to help me. They never did, I reminded myself. That thought I knew came from myself. But then, my next thoughts were unfamiliar to me. They were saying I needed to say goodbye to the kids and to Kevin, and tell them I had had a really good life. I was driving and crying, tears rolling down my cheeks. *I'd had such a good life,* I thought. *I wouldn't change a thing, but it's over.* There was no decision to make. It had been made for me by thoughts that I didn't recognize as my own. I could drive into oncoming traffic or roll my vehicle.

I could envision it; I could see it repeatedly play in my mind. I said my goodbyes to life. All I had to do was turn the wheel and cross the center line. I kept thinking, *I'll probably only get hurt. This isn't the way to do it.* At that point, there were no thoughts of calling someone, going to a hospital, texting anyone or asking anyone for help, because the thought told me it was going to happen, so there was no use.

Somehow, I managed to get myself home, and thankfully Kevin was there. If he hadn't been home, I don't know how this story would end. But when I saw him, I felt I snapped back into my reality where my thoughts became my own again. I just cried and cried and cried.

I don't think people leave this earth by suicide unless they feel like there is no other choice, and in my case, my brain was telling me I had no choice. If I had died that day, so many people would have wondered how I could possibly do that to my family. But the truth was, I wasn't in control of my thoughts or my will. It was like a heart attack in my brain that no one could control, and it could have killed me.

Later my therapist would tell me that by going to the hospital, even if no one helped me, just sitting in the waiting room could have broken the pattern. What this experience taught me was that I couldn't stop this kind of suicidal desire unless I consciously made myself do something to interrupt the pattern. I had to remind myself if I ever felt that way again to do anything I could just to make it stop.

TMS Session Twelve

The twelfth morning of TMS, I hugged my pillow tight and tried to quiet my flinching muscles with my breathing. I got lost in happy memories about time spent with my dad. He was fifty years old when I was in kindergarten, and it always frightened me that he wouldn't be there to see me grow up. He was so witty, so easy to talk to about anything, and he had always been happy with life just the way it was. He never worried about what he might be missing out on. He was simply happy to have his family, his farmwork, and his church on Sunday. Soon the memories of my fear of losing him turned to gratitude. Kevin had lost his own father at fifty, and here I was already having 40 more years than they had gotten. How grateful I was that he had been happy and healthy and an integral part of keeping our family so connected. I was truly blessed!

I'd had a dream the night before that Mom and Dad took me to Aunt Elaine's house. Whereas in my usual dream of this house the rooms were always empty, this time the house was piled full of stuff. As we were walking around, we saw beds, blankets, furniture, toys, and boxes everywhere. But nothing looked familiar to me.

Then a lady walked in and said, "What are you doing in my house? You don't have permission to be here! Get out!"

I looked over at Dad and said, "Why did you bring me here if we weren't supposed to go inside?"

He simply said, "Because you wanted to come."

When I looked at the dream during TMS, I saw Aunt Elaine.

She said, "I'm not in the house anymore. You don't have to keep looking for me there. You don't have to continue searching. I am with you. I'll always be part of you."

I told my tech what I had just experienced. She had said early on that the goal of treatment was to build new pathways in my brain, and that the work I did would cement those pathways down.

"I think your vision just now might be a sign that this is starting to happen!" she told me. "You have accepted your aunt's death, and realized that she is still in your heart and you will never lose her."

"I hope you're right," I replied. "I sometimes don't feel like anything is happening."

"Don't worry. We'll keep working on it together. Think of it this way, I am the one who is building the road, and your job is to pour the cement and then maintain it. Can you do that?"

I laughed. "I'm trying," I told her.

"Well right now, one of your main tasks is to figure out how to love yourself again."

I thought, *It's more like how to like myself, or even just tolerate myself.*

When did I stop liking myself? I didn't know, but I had to forgive myself for a lot of things, forgive and then accept my mistakes and begin to see myself as worthy. I had tried to come up with a few things that I liked about myself. One of them was my thick wavy hair that I got from my dad. But I had seen in the mirror that morning that patches of hair were coming out around my temples, likely due to the TMS. I had stared at myself in disbelief. *You mean to say that the one thing about myself that I like you are now going to take away from me?*

Self-affirmations were hard. So were getting compliments from others. If you didn't truly believe them, then how did they work? For example, if everyone around me said that they love onions, I would still hate onions, regardless of how wonderful anyone said they were.

They are so yummy!
They make food taste better!
They give everything a good flavor!

To all of that I would say, "Yuck! I will always hate onions."

So how would I get myself to love onions if I hated them so much? Maybe I would have to do it step by step. (By the way, I do not ever plan on doing this.) First maybe I'd have to sit near the onion bag without feeling disgust. Then maybe I'd have a look at it and hold it in my hands. Then maybe I would cut a piece of, sit with it, smell it (after I stop puking!) Then maybe eventually I would taste it. But I had a strong feeling that after all of this I would still hate it!

What if I did something different with the onion, knowing already how much I hated it? What if I coated it in batter and deep fried it and then ate it? Yep, I would like that! But it would still be the same onion that I had held in my hand and smelled and then wanted to puke. Could I be the same onion that other people loved and I hated, but then turn myself into something that I would finally accept? In other words, if I reviewed all my flaws and saw at least some positives in them, would that be like the coated batter and the deep fry?

During the second part of treatment, I started thinking about how I thought I was finally ready to let go of some of the sadness I've felt about how I ended up somewhere so different than I had wanted to be. The truth was, if we hadn't ended up living on the farm, my daughter Kierra – an old soul – would have been lost in a city. I thought about how much of a natural she was on the farm. When we had a couple of terrible snowstorms one April during calving season, we had to bring calves inside. Kierra slept in the kitchen under the table with the calves. Sometimes she was up at 5:00 a.m., getting a bottle ready to start feeding one of the orphans. She had always loved this house and this yard as if it was something that she had known for a long time was the place she was meant to be. God had a plan for us to be here when Kevin's dad died at such a young age. We were the lucky ones whose souls were picked to flourish on the farm and love it with all our being.

There were so many other things I loved about where we'd ended up. Although Kevin had never completely approved of me wanting to take the kids travelling every year, I knew how important it was for them to experience the world, and for me to get to experience it through their eyes. Our holidays would be Kevin's compromise to me. Our children got to experience the best of both worlds – the farm, the work ethic, the budget, the time with animals, along with camping, the lake, and lifelong memories of all the trips we took them on. Because of the variety of what they've seen, they have a different perspective of their world. They are aware of homelessness, dictatorships, and corruption. They saw the poorest of the poor, and they know that where we live and where we came from is something to be grateful for. I love that between Kevin and myself we were able to make them into such well-rounded individuals.

There is no ounce of me that wishes it were any different, and I am grateful that God's plan wasn't my plan, and I can let that rest now. Our children and I are exactly where we are supposed to be.

TMS Session Thirteen

Kevin had tried over the years to get me to avoid the news at all costs.

Every time I would even bring up a news article, he would say, "I told you to stop reading that stuff." Gesturing out the window he would tell me, "This is our world. This is all you need to worry about."

Somehow though, I could never truly avoid delving into terrible news articles and being horrified by a true crime story. I knew I wasn't supposed to read the news, but listening to a *Crime Junkies* podcast for eight hours on the way to and from Calgary didn't count, right? I always came up with excuses.

What puzzled me was the way the press dealt with the mental health aspect of so many crimes. On one episode of *The View*, they talked about how mental illness is a common denominator in so many shootings in the States. *They snapped for various reasons and then killed 15 school-age children. They must have had serious mental problems!* This frustrated me so much. How could we end the stigma of mental illness when it all got painted with one brush like this?

Recently I was scrolling TikTok for some light entertainment, funny cat videos, fashion, celebrity gossip, that kind of thing. If one or two crime articles happened to show up, I couldn't help it, could I? I read them and they horrified me. A father had murdered his common law wife, niece, and three children in a horrifying manner, and had burned them. They had lived about four hours from here. Without digging too far into the case, I noted that it said at one point, *Anyway, he had depression and anxiety.* Boom! There it was – depression and anxiety, the double whammy. When people found out about my depression and anxiety, never mind the violent images of OCD, would I be painted with that same brush?

I couldn't help but think of the animated film *Zootopia*. In the movie, the predators were living peacefully with the mammals, but suddenly they accidentally took a drug that made them turn savage. Until everyone figured that out, the other creatures in the town thought it was in the predators' DNA to be violent. They started losing their jobs, everyone was afraid of them, and no one wanted to sit beside one. Even though it only happened to four or five predators, essentially all the millions of predators were segregated, isolated, and could no longer live peacefully in Zootopia. It was so easy for the rest of the society to believe that they were all terrible, turn against them, and accept that maybe their brains were faulty.

Did that happen in our society? Did we shun people with mental illness? I think about my fear of snapping, and then my childhood fear that one day my uncle would come over and kill us. I certainly do not intend to paint everyone with schizophrenia with that same brush, and I hope I make that clear. I certainly don't want society in general to think of all mental illness as the cause of so many tragedies.

I learned later that the case of the father murdering his family was not just depression and anxiety. He had suffered years of trauma as a child, had many aggressive attacks on record, had experienced substance abuse and was an addict. How do we stop this from happening to another family?

I used my TMS treatment time today to remind myself that those children who were killed and burned by their father were not my children, and again, just like the Tori Stafford case or Paul Bernardo's murders, the victims' lives were not my cross to bear. They each had their own stories, their own loved ones and their own soul's journey, and it was not mine.

But my family hasn't been untouched by violent crime. One year around Valentine's Day, my brother was on his way to get some movie tickets for his daughters for a gift. As he was walking into the mall, a complete stranger randomly attacked him, stabbing him five times. Thankfully my brother was wearing a thick Canada goose jacket, but a few of the cuts did puncture his lungs. The person who attacked him had a long history of aggression, and had been in and out of jail. He ended up getting convicted of aggressive assault, but wasn't even charged with attempted murder! Because of some time he had already served, he basically was out in a year. It's sickening that nothing more is done in these cases, which is one of the reasons these crimes keep increasing.

If we do nothing to help heal childhood trauma and substance abuse, senseless murders will continue. If you are doing nothing about the signs that lead up to someone committing suicide or murder, you are doing nothing. But it would help lessen the number of killings in the United States if they had a ban on assault rifles. Can you imagine if instead of a knife, the man who attacked my brother had used an assault gun, and taken out forty or fifty others as well? By letting people have access to those types of guns, you are increasing the death toll.

***

As soon as I started to feel a wee bit better, I took on too much, as is my habit. As my Fluoxetine was starting to kick in, even after all the terrible suicidal thoughts and a near miss on the highway, I still pressed onward. I knew I needed to cut back on work, so I went down to four days a week. The rest of our life was already so chaotic, between the farm and the kids, that I felt like cutting back on work would relieve some stress.

Fall was always busy on the farm, with a particular rush to it, because things had to get done before the ground froze. It made everyone feel like they had to hustle, and anxieties always started running high around this time. Our family was always a little chaotic, even when it wasn't fall season. The best I can do to describe what it is like in our house is to imagine all of us are loud and have ADHD. We all cut each other off when we are speaking, the loudest person gets the floor, and things have to be repeated ten times because there's always someone not listening at the time. Our mornings are extremely hectic. Kevin and I also aren't early birds; we are more sleep-until-the-last-minute type of people. Then we struggle to get Brant up and going, get his breakfast and find all he needs for his school day. Ava adds to the noise by also being late after she has changed her outfit five times, and we all bump into each other in the kitchen trying to make our way out. After school and supper are very similar, as we assess what happened during the day, what farm chores need to be done, what schoolwork needs to be done and negotiate over who is going to clean the kitchen.

We had nothing planned for the September long weekend. Ava had been bugging me about fostering some animals. I had continuously said no, but just before the long weekend, a litter of twelve kittens was being taken from a home of thirty cats. They were in deplorable condition. I said that I thought we could manage nine in our barn. I knew Kevin and the rest of the world would think I was crazy, but I knew Brant and Ava would love cuddling and looking after these sweet little things that needed our help. There was a large section of the barn cornered off when the girls had rabbits, and it would suit the kittens fine.

    It started off pretty well. The kids were happy in their roles as caretakers, and the kittens were cute. But then some of the kittens started getting sick. One night after supper, I called for Brant to come with me to go do the nighttime check. He was playing in the sink, and rushing to join me, left the tap running and the sink plugged. We went to the barn and found a kitten that had died. We found a box for it, then tried to take care of the others. When we got home, there was water running down the hallway. I shut off the tap and started to throw towels down and then I went downstairs and saw it had gone through the ceiling and the carpet was wet in the basement. Again I hurried with towels to start saving the carpet. I felt so guilty not knowing what might have happened to that kitten. I phoned the rescue to tell them about losing the kitten, and knew that they were thinking I was an awful person. Then I felt even more guilty calling Kevin to tell him that on my watch, Brant left the water running and there was a flood. I wanted to bury myself in a hole.

    A couple of days later, another kitten passed away. He was one of the kids' favorites, so it was very sad. There was another kitten who looked close to death, so I called the rescue again. I asked them what we should do, and they suggested Pedialyte and said to get them all on antibiotics. So we dropped Pedialyte in the very sick kitten's mouth every hour. There would be moments where he would become stiff and fall right on his head. We were certain he wouldn't make the night. Ava got up religiously every couple of hours to make sure he got Pedialyte and soft food. Thankfully he started to recover.

    Then it came time to bury the two kittens who had died. We wanted a proper burial for them, as we were incredibly sad with what happened to them. Brant picked a spot by some trees, and he and his friend carried the kittens in their box on the electric scooter to the funeral. We had an electric fence, and I had to step on it while Kevin dug the hole. When the service was over, the electric fence had a lot of tension and I ended up tripping, falling backwards and landing by the fresh burial. Brant quickly asked if I was okay, while Kevin laughed, and I said just leave me here. Sometimes my life felt more like a movie than real life.

    Weeks went by and I would take our kitties every week for adoption weekends. I took them to school on my day off and Brant was thrilled. When I was on work trips, Ava was running the show for them. One night as I was coming home from Regina, a van coming towards me lost their front tire and the tire flew into my lane. I was more worried about the van though, since it had lost control. We were both going over 100. The tire narrowly missed my windshield and the van stayed on his side. When I pulled over, he was in shock and so was I. He said he promised he wasn't trying to kill me. I thought, Don't *worry, it wouldn't even shock me. Someone is always trying to kill me, whether it's my own thoughts or someone in my nightmares.*

    I had started to have nightmares again. Usually if I was stressed, my nightmares repeated themselves: there's a gunman in the room, or a bomb, or any type of killer, and I run and hide to all different locations. I try hiding under mattresses, scurrying to closets, attics – anywhere I can conceal myself. Then the killer catches me and starts to shoot or stab me, or the bomb goes off. I always wake up just before it happens, in a panic with my heart racing.

    But one night I had a nightmare that was different. I dreamed that there was something wrong with my body. I had noticed in June one of my breasts was larger than the other, and I could feel something on the side of it. In the nightmare I found out that it was cancer. This scared me so I went to the doctor. After examining me, he said he was fairly sure it wasn't much to worry about, but he knew that any change is something that warrants investigation, especially since I was on add-back estrogen. So, he said he would recommend I go for a mammogram, and that they should be able to schedule it within a week.

    Nope! He was wrong – the pope had a better chance of going to a Halloween party than I had of getting a mammogram in our hospital in a week. I was told it would be more like a couple of months. We were going away on a family trip to Mexico in November, and I desperately wanted some answers before we went. My anxiety was high, and with all the health issues I'd had with my endometriosis and ischemic colitis, I was gun shy of our medical system. So I made some calls and I was able to get a mammogram scheduled in Calgary within three days. All I had to do was hop on a plane. I was going to Regina for meetings anyway, but I'd have to cancel the one day of meetings and just fly from there to Calgary the day for the mammogram.

The morning I woke up for my mammogram, it was supposed to snow and be terribly icy and I was not looking forward to that driving in Calgary. The mammogram was typical, and I was in and out of there fast, it did seem there was nothing pressing urgent before I left Calgary, so I was able to make it to my meetings in Regina.

When I need to make appearances or get things accomplished, my energy runs on high. At one of the meetings in Regina, we did a roundtable where you had to describe yourself in one word. Given my hyper state at the time, I labelled myself as *happy*. As my turn ended, I suddenly thought to myself, *WTF is wrong with you? Happy?? That is your word for yourself?*

It was the only thing I could think of at the time. I knew I couldn't say *organized*, or *energetic*, I'm not *smart*, anyone can say *kind*, so I guess I'm *happy*? What a crock! Probably the craziest part is that most people believed it. There I was, worried about my mammogram, taking flights around the countryside, driving in ice and snow and I was happy! "How embarrassing," I thought to myself. "Some of them surely have to see right through that."

I'm an egg ready to break into pieces in any moment. I have secrets a mile long, I'm an imposter, an impersonator. No one actually knows me. Sure, I talk a lot and leave little clues, but no one knew how dark my brain actually was.

I went and saw the doctor when I got back home. He suggested the results were a bit suspicious and wanted a surgeon to look into getting a biopsy. I was okay with that answer, as it was calcifications and the radiologist had written to be seen again in a year. I knew my doctor was cautious though and had caught other cancers that radiologists had blown off. But I was thankful that I felt that I could go on our family trip and not worry about anything physical or medical.

TMS Session Fourteen

On the morning of TMS day fourteen, I was feeling pretty good. Kevin had been cracking a bunch of jokes when we were all getting ready, and I was feeling almost a little giddy. Then my TMS tech asked me what I had done the day before, just making conversation.

"I had a good lunch with my mom and dad," I told her.

But then out of nowhere, *bam*, the waterworks began. Tears started pouring from my eyes. "My ninety-year-old father seemed sad yesterday when I was explaining all the years that I went through this illness. He said, 'We didn't know! You always looked so happy.'"

I didn't cry at the time he said it, or even think it was sad, but suddenly it was bringing me to tears. Maybe it was the realization that there are so many things about people you can never know.

"I'm sorry. I don't know why I can't stop crying," I told my tech.

"It isn't your fault," she said. "All this came out right now for a reason, and you should try not to be hard on yourself about it."

I imagined his sad, weathered brown eyes and just kept crying.

During treatment, my brain was trying to process how I'd done this my whole life long. If my mom and dad, whom I love dearly, all my family, and all my friends had not seen any signs in my smiling, happy self that something was wrong, then how would we see the signs in so many others who suffer in silence? To say that my family would have been shocked if I had taken my life last July would be an understatement; they would have been blown away.

I thought that maybe it had something to do with how I'd always felt like I needed to make people around me be happy. To do that, I often had to hide how I felt inside. If someone could be a people pleaser from birth, it would be me. I've lived and thrived off pleasing people. It was my drug. I couldn't think of anything worse than someone not liking me. If I were to stand up for myself, or tell someone how I really felt, they might not like me. Some may call it tactful; some may call it reading a room. I called it being a people-pleasing chameleon.

Here's an example: I don't like hunting. I have no earthly idea why someone would want to shoot an animal and hang it up for show. I understand if you need to kill to have meat for food, but I don't get killing so you can have a trophy. When I see a beautiful animal running across the field, I never think, *I should hunt that down until the fear pours out of its insides, and then I should shoot it and put it on a wall to show that I have a gun and it doesn't.* I think chasing coyotes with snowmobiles until they die from their last fearful breath is horrible. But would I say that out loud in this farming and hunting community? Absolutely not. I would say, "Did you get your buck? Good for you!" Because that is what I am supposed to say if I want to fit into society where I live. Societal norms require that we learn to read the room wherever we are. The only way to make friends instead of enemies is to understand that people have different interests, and I may not agree with all of theirs and they may not agree with all of mine.

But during treatment, I started to think that maybe I needed to look at the line between fitting in with what society expected of me and remaining true to myself, especially within our immediate family. It's always been very important to us that everyone get along, and both Kevin and I would do pretty much anything to keep the peace. I didn't think that this was a bad thing, but it did take a lot of give and take and a lot of people pleasing from everyone involved. But recently I had started to wonder if it was all a charade. Had we ever really gotten to the heart of what was causing problems when we've dealt with things in our lives? It was kind of like the storage room – until the glass jar fell and shattered, everyone was okay with it being just where it was, hidden up on a shelf. Sometimes I craved deepness though. I craved authenticity. I was raised to be good and quiet, and that no one wanted to hear you talk about your feelings. I think most of our generation was raised that way. But while I accepted that, I also found myself wanting to know the people I love more deeply. I wanted to know what made their heart ache, what made their heart sing with joy, and everything in between. I wanted to be able to talk about deep stuff without anyone getting defensive but just listening to each other. I wanted to know why you might disagree with me, because in that way I can start to understand your point of view. I wanted to grow and learn from you. I wanted to do more than just play games and laugh and drink and eat until we pass out. Of course, I did love the games and having fun, but I really wanted that deeper connection.

Last year I told a work colleague I had just met more about myself in a two-hour ride than anyone in my family or friends knew. Why? I guess it felt safe. She didn't know my happy, smiling image, I had nothing to shatter and disappoint her with.

***

Well we had made it to the week of our vacation to Mexico. Going on a trip in the fall with a farmer is like taking a fish out of water and asking it to breathe on its own. Fall was always a difficult time, and in true Kevin fashion, he had decided to do day and night of land levelling with his scraper the week before we left. The words, "It has to be done now, when it's dry!" or "It has to be done now, when it's wet!" or when the sun shines, or when the first drops of rain fall or when the ground is just starting to freeze, or when there is a storm coming, are words that every farm wife hears. Everything either stops or starts because of the weather. And when it starts, you better friggen hustle!

So there we were, a day before we were supposed to leave. Kevin had about ten hours of chores to do before we left at 4:00 a.m. And if things went like they usually did, he would find about five hours more. There was a terrible ice storm predicted, and flashes of red were all over the weather app, warning of the dangerous conditions. Ava's boyfriend was going with us, and his parents called us, worried about the weather forecast.

"Please," they begged, "won't you consider leaving the night before? We will pay for the hotel."

I had thought the same thing, but Kevin wouldn't hear of it. It wasn't the cost of a hotel; it was the amount of work he had to do.

I was walking on eggshells around him. "Maybe I should just go the night before and take Brant and the other kids, and you can come with Kierra at 4:00 a.m.," I suggested.

Nope, he wouldn't hear of it.

"There is just too much to do here," he told me. But then he conceded a little. "Okay, we can leave at 11:00 and sleep in the car at the airport. That should help us avoid the worst of the storm."

I tried to go to sleep, completely stressed out about the highway getting shut down, or the flight not being able to take off. But I only dozed for a few hours, if that. We were taking two vehicles to the airport, and I was driving one of them. It was extremely icy, and my knuckles were white on the wheel. Thankfully after about an hour of driving it started to get better, and eventually we made it to the flight in time. I could finally relax!

I had been looking forward to this vacation for two years. We usually travel in November, and hadn't been able to go anywhere last year because I was at the Mayo Clinic. I loved beach vacations; they were my favorite. I couldn't wait to smell the humid air, see the pretty flowers, put on my bathing suit and plunk in a chair. We were staying at a beautiful resort, and after three days we'd found a bunch of favorite spots to spend the day. We went on a catamaran one day, and I got out to swim in the crystal-clear blue water. It was so beautiful, and felt like silk, so I took advantage and swam a long time. Unfortunately, when the attendant tried to get me back into the boat, he had a hard time. He ended up squeezing my life jacket so tight that I got a rope burn on my chest. Just a little something to add to my war wounds and another trip souvenir that I was sure the breast surgeon I'd see in a couple weeks would be impressed with!

We were having a great time. But on day three, as we were eating our Italian supper in the hotel restaurant, my stomach started to do a lot of gurgling, I knew something explosive was about to happen, and ran out of the restaurant with my cheeks clenched as hard as I could clench them. Thankfully I made it back to the room in time. I felt like I had to throw up, but I knew from experience that if I could just take some Gravol, do my meditations, and get through this, hopefully it would pass. I tried my best during meditation to listen to lyrics to songs to make myself think about other things, and eventually I fell asleep. But around 3:00 a.m., I woke up about to vomit. I ran to the bathroom with my hand over my mouth, and I started throwing up. I was holding my hand so tight that the vomit was going up my nose and choking me while spraying on the floor and open suitcases, I got to the bathroom and threw up everywhere. I also had nonstop diarrhea. I didn't bother waking Kevin, because this would in fact make him throw up and possibly never sleep with me again. I took the white hotel towels and started mopping everything up. Then I got in the shower to clean my hair, my nose, it was even in my ears. My pajamas and underwear are ruined and after I am done mopping it all up with the towels, I took it all out to the deck. I saved some towels and used them to scrub down the bathroom. Then I put everything I thought could be saved into the bathtub to soak. I would see if the stains could be removed tomorrow. I crawled back into bed and honestly almost had to laugh. I'd been through all kinds of vomiting episodes but this one reached heights I couldn't have even imagined.

    The next day I was weak and very irritable that I had to spend a day of our big vacation in bed. Brant and Kevin brought me Jello and buns every few hours, and at least I could keep them down. I soon was on the mend, and the rest of the trip was pretty good. Unfortunately, what I was sick with ended up being a stomach bug, and it hit nearly everyone on the trip. Driving home, everyone had diarrhea, and alternated jumping out of the car to go on the side of the road, with the few McDonald's napkins I had in the car. Our family vacations are anything but dull!

TMS Session Fifteen

I pushed myself to get going in TMS today. I yawned, and struggled thinking about the first few minutes, when I couldn't get control of my hand-twitching until I settled into my breathing. I hated that part. I started my affirmations: I am strong, I am brave, I am courageous. But I was surprised when I started feeling a different vibe. As I repeated them, I started to think about how I feel about being strong, and what that means. It seemed like throughout my TMS journey, the affirmations have fallen on my own deaf ears. Especially the idea of being strong. I always wanted to be strong, but what I never wanted to be was someone who was confrontational. I also worried about revealing too much about how I was feeling, in fear that people would think they had to walk around on eggshells to not hurt my feelings. It reminded me of the movie *Barbie,* and the monologue about how difficult it is to be a woman. How do you tell people how you really feel without looking like "poor me"? How do you tell them they hurt your feelings when you don't want to look sensitive? How do you blow up at someone for saying terrible things to you but not look like you're crazy?

    I think a lot of it has to do with our obsession with trying to be perfect. I had always wanted to be perfect, for myself yes, but also for my parents so they could boast about their perfect university kids. But my family didn't make me feel this way; I made myself feel this way, because I felt like if I wasn't perfect like my siblings, I was a failure. I searched for everyone's approval but my own. Isn't that the problem with our social media today? We continue to be attracted to perfection, whatever we think that is, and when we feel it can never be attained, we pretend.

    Who is that person we imagine with the big fancy house, the cottage at the lake, the children with high marks who's on all the sports teams, the Cadillac Escalade, the perfect flowing hair, the size six body with the perfect amount of curve and abs? This imaginary person eats healthy, runs, does yoga at dawn, makes cookies for school, never forgets a friend's birthday, always remembers the library books. They put heart-shaped sandwiches with notes in lunches, have all the latest styles of clothes and shoes, make their kids brush their teeth, help their kids with homework, take their kids on all kinds of travel experiences. Their husband is gorgeous and dotes on them and the whole family, he's kind and generous, fun and outgoing, volunteers for everything and is always happy and smiling.

Do you know anyone who is perfect? I think I might know them, at least I've seen them on Instagram. Oh wait, was that the TikTokker who was just charged with child abuse? Hmmm, there may be more to this story! Or was that the one whose husband is on Tinder and who sleeps with anything with breasts? Or maybe it was that beautiful girl who was on *The Bachelor*…oh wait, she committed suicide last week. He is addicted to cocaine, she is addicted to morphine, he sleeps around, she sleeps around, he spends all their money on stupid stuff, she spends all their money on stupid stuff, he does extreme discipline with the kids, she does zero discipline with the kids, he has cancer, she has multiple sclerosis, he is addicted to work, she only wants to go out to party, he wants to be a swinger, she doesn't want to be a swinger, he wants her to look after herself and lose weight, she wants him to lose his beer belly, she wants diamonds, he just wants sex, and on and on and on.

There is more to everyone's story. No matter how high the penthouse and how breathtaking we imagine the view from the big windows, we never know what is really happening up there. We think they have it all, and we try to get it for ourselves, but in doing this, we are never happy. Seeking perfection is like being on a hamster wheel. You run and run, but you can never attain, because it doesn't exist.

We collectively must agree that there is no perfection. As my friend Shelly says, "There is no prize at the end for excelling at life." The beauty is that we are a part of writing the story, and we can change it at any time. Although we don't control the beginning or the end, we do have a chance to do everything that makes us happy. Regardless of whether we have a short story, a tragic story, or a long story, what we do within that story is ours. We can't take away hurts, grief, loss, suffering but in the middle we can survive. We can't be perfect, but we can do the things that make our souls soar.

So when the world gets hard and you feel like you can't make it one more day, remember your soul. It's in you and it's been there all along. It will send you all kinds of brain and body signals and when you are ready to listen it will tell you the way. It will lead the way out of the darkness; you just have to listen to it.

***

Eventually I followed through with my doctor about the biopsy he had recommended. But as it turned out, the surgeon thought there was not quite enough evidence to suggest that I needed one. He said he wanted another mammogram done in the next month or so. I decided to phone to see when they had scheduled my appointment, and was shocked to hear that I was number 209 on the waitlist. They told me it might be another six to ten months before I got an appointment. I called a private clinic about four hours away, and they said they could see me within the month. While I was happy to have the appointment, I could feel my anger bubbling over. We pay enormous taxes in order to have access to "free" healthcare. But what good is it if you can never get in to see a doctor? Where was all our money going?

Somewhere in between worrying about my mammogram, I kept receiving calls from my doctor's office. When I finally got in touch with them, they told me that the night I went to the emergency room, they had tested my liver enzymes as part of the blood work. My doctor told me that he wanted to retest them, because something "didn't look right."

I didn't say anything to them, but I couldn't help but think about how that was the night I was contemplating making a plan for suicide, so of course my body was in a state of fight or flight. I was shaking, my heart was pounding, my head hurt and I was throwing up in the bathroom. I would imagine all that would affect the results of the liver test. But for me it was just another thing I had to deal with – going to get my blood retested. In addition to that I had to send my request to Saskatoon for the mammogram and call Calgary and get my October images sent to my primary doctor's office. Anyone going through illnesses knows that it is a full-time job just keeping up with all those demands, never mind the anxiety that goes with waiting for tests, and waiting for results.

Sometimes I feel like I preoccupy myself living my lie, complaining on social media about things, worrying about my health, just so I don't have to face the brutal fact that I am going for transcranial magnetic stimulation on a daily basis to battle depression and OCD and to get rid of violent harmful thoughts and self-loathing.

There! I said it out loud in writing! Maybe one day I can say it out loud to the whole world and help other people who could benefit from hearing it.

TMS Session Sixteen

Besides the first few days of TMS, this was the hardest one in a long time. I wasn't quite sure what brought it on, but I didn't have a good sleep the night before. I'd had a nightmare that I was wheeling around pieces of dead babies in a carriage, looking for a place to dispose of them. I ended up dropping them down something that resembled a laundry chute, but then I realized that they would get stuck in there and eventually rot and smell and then everyone would know they were there and find out it was me. I woke up sad and confused.

I had thought about my miscarriage the other day, and it seemed to me that my brain was revisiting this event in my nightmare and trying to process it. I couldn't fall back asleep, and since it was 5:00 a.m., I did what do most people do at 5:00 a.m. when they can't sleep: start googling medical questions! It had been bothering me that my ALT liver enzymes had been going up for the last few years. My gastrologist had thought it had to do with fatty liver, but my liver scan showed that the fatty liver was very mild. So I pondered why the ALT enzymes kept increasing in my blood, you know because I went to Harvard medical school and all, and could easily read some case studies where this had happened.

In any case, I finally ended up falling asleep for a bit longer, having gotten zero answers. In the morning when I was putting on my bra, the one side was tight, even peeking out the bottom and the other side had lots of extra space. Of course, this added to my anxieties about the second mammogram and biopsy that I was waiting to have scheduled. So I likely had a lot of anxieties built up before I sat down for TMS.

Honestly I can barely remember the first half of the session, because the second one was so horrifying it completely overshadowed everything else. When the magnets started to hit, I began to use my script to try to work myself up. That day I was going to try to imagine some objects that scare me, and look at what they were actually used for. I started with the knife, and imagined it cutting an orange, since that's what knives are used for. But in seconds I was slitting my wrists with it, then I plunged it into my stomach and thighs.

Okay, that didn't work. I decided to try a fork. This fork is something I can use for supper. But the fork flew into my head, puncturing my forehead and causing bleeding all around my brain. After that my hand started to twitch, and my tech told me that my face looked like I was in great distress. So I thought I'd look for a spoon. Surely there was nothing dangerous about a spoon. I put the spoon in my coffee, then reached up and gouged out both of my eyes. Blood was dripping down my face.

Now I really was in great distress. Was there anything in the kitchen that wasn't dangerous? I grabbed some plastic spatulas, but then started forcing them down my throat. I got upset and flew into a rage. I picked up the fridge and threw it on top of myself. It wasn't enough. I got the stove and smashed it on top of myself. The glass broke and I started using it to slice open my neck.

And the magnets stopped.

I pulled out my ear plugs and looked at my tech.

"That was the worst of all my days here," I told her.

She looked at me kindly. "Well it is progress. We're pulling everything out and trying to change your thinking around. The electric current has to move and create other pathways. It can be painful."

I thought, "Well, maybe," but I was completely unsettled.

I drove home and tears started to flow. "Am I regressing? Will I ever break this?" I thought. I had seemed to be doing well, but now I felt like a deflated balloon that was stuck on the heat register and kept bouncing, but was slowly deflating and dying.

Would I ever get better? All I wanted to do was go to bed and never come out. I wanted to hide, I wanted to run, but there was nowhere to go. I had to face myself all day, but at least I could sleep at night and get a break from myself. But then I had to wake up and face myself again. I felt so drained, like I had been punched and kicked into a curb. Friends tried to help, offering well wishes, but they didn't really help.

Then Kevin said something that really upset me, "I'm wondering if you even want these thoughts to leave."

That made me lose my mind. I envisioned myself throwing my coffee cup at his head. I had done everything! I did everything they told me to do. I took my meds. I went through the TMS shit every day. How dare he tell me that I didn't want the thoughts to go away. I crawled back into bed again and just stared at the wall. I wished I could find a safe space where I could get up later and try again.

But at least I could say I made it one more day, and as the saying goes, "It isn't until it is the darkest that you start to see the light." Please Lord, let the sun come out tomorrow. Let my gracious, kind soul get me through until my brain begins to heal.

***

I had been writing a lot in my journal over the previous few days. I'd decided that one thing I have realized from all these treatments is how much I have fought, and how my fight has taught me invaluable lessons that I hope others can use. By sharing my story, I want to give others who suffer through similar pain a head start in their journey towards healing. Here is what I have learned.

My advice for women who have had C sections or D and C and unexplained pelvic pain – I am not a doctor, but my guess is that you have endometriosis. As long as you have your period it will continue to grow. Try taking Mirena, and if it works for you, try to get it to buy you enough time to get to menopause. It had no major side effects on my mood, as it doesn't have a high dose of estrogen in it. However, it should stop or minimize your cycle so that your endometriosis stops growing. But if pelvic pain continues to be unexplained, press your doctors for an ultrasound to see about cysts. If nothing shows up there, it doesn't mean you don't have endometriosis. Press them hard and get to an endometriosis specialist, because it can't be seen on ultrasound or CT. MRI is possible, but the only fool-proof method is to open you up. Don't be afraid to get answers if you continually are going to emergency with pain and they are giving you Toradol and sending you home. Don't let them make you give up. Get to a gynecologist and get sent on to a specialist, so that you can avoid my ten-year path of pain. I also think the delay in getting treated is what led to my bowel endometriosis, which I believe led to the ischemic colitis.

If you are trying to have a baby and you have endometriosis – Remember that even at stage four, I was able to conceive, so there is hope. However, my advice is to fully be prepared with a back up plan and make peace with it, whatever it is. After that, leave it up to the master plan. If there is a little soul waiting for you, it will happen, and if there is another soul in another home that also has been waiting for you, don't overthink it. I know this is easier said than done, but try to make peace with it.

If you have had a bowel attack with stabbing pain, diarrhea and blood – You must not only get to a hospital, but you will more than likely have to press them to find out why this is happening. Don't wait until they have to cut a piece of your colon out. Go to specialists but also remember, if you have any similarities to my case, high estrogen, birth control pills, and/or endometriosis could be to blame. You can fight it by figuring out how to reduce the estrogen, drinking lots and lots of fluid, taking care not to get constipated, walking, and focusing on self-care.

If you are a young person and you have started having obsessive unwanted thoughts that are debilitating your home life, school life, or work life – Please tell someone. Your first step is simply to tell one person and get some support. Then fight to get to a doctor as soon as you can. Fight to get into a psychiatrist's office where they can help you. Fight for a treatment that is right for you. If you want, I can be the first person you talk to. You will be met with a kind heart, a loving ear and someone who knows the darkest horrors of this disease, so you can't scare me. My mental health journey is far from over, but I hope you will use it to realize that you must not hold in your secret. There is much more help now and far less stigma than there were years ago. I'm a realist and I know not all lives can be saved from this intrusive disease that takes over your brain and tells you lies about yourself. However, with continued education we can continue to fight, and we can live very successful lives in whatever way success looks to you. My wise sister-in-law Tammy once told me, "Success does not determine happiness; happiness determines success."

To those who have lost someone to suicide or continue to accept the myth that those who consider suicide are selfish – Try to accept that your loved one had nowhere to go. Their brain turned on them and they really had no choice. There was no second thoughts, only the lies the disease told them. Their brain had what sometimes compare to an aneurism that day, and it was nothing that could have been stopped. Your loved one should never be remembered as selfish. They loved you more than anything in the world, but as an aneurism can take someone in their sleep, this disease did, too. You don't have to second guess how things might have been different if you had done something different. It was going to happen the way it did, and having been at the depths of that horror, I can tell you they are finally at peace.

For those who are watching someone suffer from OCD and depression – Just be there for them. Don't overthink what you say or what you do, just love the person. Check in and help them get the help that they need, and then check in again. Once they are in treatment, the healing is up to them. Remember that you are not responsible for that. Like cancer, the disease will ravage them and tear them to shreds, and there is no chemotherapy or treatment that can save them. They will go in and out of remission and fight this for as long as they are able. A disease is a disease, and it can be treatable or terminal. I am here to give hope to those who find it to be treatable, but I don't want to shame anyone else who find that it wasn't treatable for their loved one. Unfortunately, in life there are those uncertainties I've talked about. But while there are no guarantees, there is a lot that people who suffer can do. They can help others, for one thing. But they can also focus on enjoying every sunset, every bubble bath, every child's laugh, and every campfire. You and your loved one just have to keep believing that you will get through this. So whether it's grief you suffer or your own disease, there will be those glimmers in the darkest depths of hopelessness where you will feel a hug, see a smile, laugh at a joke, and know you can do this for one more day, one step at a time.

For those unaligned in their marriages with much hurt and much resentment – During one of our heated battles, I texted Kevin the words from Diamond Rio, "I'll start walking your way, you start walking mine, we'll meet in the middle by the old Georgia pine, we'll gain a lot of ground, cause we'll both give a little and there ain't no road too long, when you meet in the middle." If you can live in each other's shoes for just a few minutes, it is possible to love someone more than you ever thought possible. Both parties have to meet in the middle though, not just one. And while this has helped our journey, I know that it doesn't work for everyone. But explore other options, and keep your mind open.

    For those who have always hated the way that you look – Do some work on exploring triggers from the past and make peace with them. Go to therapy. Love yourself from the day of your first memory to the day of your last. You have done amazing things, and your eight-year-old self and your ninety-year-old self only want one thing for you – to be happy. So attack the hate you have for yourself head on; you will be surprised when you start digging just how strong you are. Begin to love yourself unconditionally as all those around you do. If you hear mean voices instead of unconditional supportive ones, then break the mold and stand up to them and your inner critic. I know you are strong enough. Just believe.

TMS Session Seventeen

Breakdown or Breakthrough?

It seemed to me that the good, the bad and the ugly, the anger and the sadness, and just about all my emotions were starting to flow out of me like a leaking garden hose. It was hard to contain at times, and putting a piece of electrical tape over it to stop the leak wasn't doing shit. I felt raw, like my skin was exposed, and the hot sun or the cold wind was making it burn. I'd been asked a lot if I thought I was making progress and the truth was, I didn't have a clue. I wondered if it would have hurt this much if I had just kept going on autopilot – working, excelling at life, being a good mom, and stuffing these emotions where the sun don't shine. I was too far in it though to turn back.

As I drove to TMS today, I wasn't thinking about crashing into oncoming traffic, but as I passed a big farm implement with its cultivator wings up, I thought, *Please God, let the wing break and smash me into a thousand pieces.* While I wouldn't have done anything intentionally, the thought did cross my mind that the pain would be over. My family wouldn't suffer as much, because it would have been the result of an accident.

Then a car up ahead coming towards me swerved on the road as the driver adjusted his morning cup of coffee. Again, I said, *Please come into my lane, please just drive right into me and smash me to smithereens.*

By the time I arrived, I was of course in tears. In the waiting room I felt so desperate I started googling residential facilities for people with OCD. Was there a place where they could put me in a rubber room, where no one would have any expectations of me? Someone would serve me breakfast at 9:00, at 10:00 I would do yoga, at 11:00 I would do some journalling, then it would be lunch that I would be served, then I would have a therapy session, more time to write, a swim in the pool at 4:00, supper at 6:00 and a walk around the lake at 8:00. Every day I would just work on me, and it would be perfection! I'd come back healthy and well rested, ready to get back to my routine and work. Wouldn't I?

When I got in the treatment room, the tech asked me as she did every morning where my mood was on a scale of 1 to

10. I said it was at a 1. Certainly that was not progress, and certainly I was horrified to let down everyone who was rooting for me. I told her how I had been fantasizing about going to a treatment facility.

"If I could just take a little break like that, I could get strong enough to start the fight again," I said. "I think if I could just have that time for myself, everything would be so much better."

She looked at me with understanding in her eyes. "But Michelle, remember that your life and your struggles would still be there when you got back. The pressure and expectations you put on yourself won't go away just because you went away on vacation for a while. In fact, they would probably feel worse." She patted my shoulder. "I understand. We'd all love to be locked away in a padded room for a while. But the truth is, you must live with your illness to heal from it and carry on with real life."

"How do I do that right now," I cried. "How do I keep up when my brain feels literally like it's being fried with an electric current? How do I survive the exhaustion and all the emotion it's making me have? I feel like I cannot possibly keep up with my life."

She had an answer for me. "Boundaries," she said. "Just one word, but it means a whole lot of things. You must learn to put your own needs before those of others right now. You must set boundaries about what you can and can't do, what you will and won't do."

"But that feels selfish," I told her.

"Is it selfish though to put yourself first? Do you really believe that?"

Of course, everyone would say no, but then again, they aren't the ones having things taken away from them or the ones having to do more work when I say I can't do it any longer. Does life stop because I don't feel well? Who picks up the slack?

***

My weekend was a roller coaster of emotions, and I couldn't decide if the word to use was *breakdown* or *breakthrough*. I found it way easier to think about boundaries than to actually lay them out for my family. My people-pleasing gene finds it hard to stand up for what I need. But this weekend I did just that.

It started out with me wanting to have a calm weekend. I had planned to take a peaceful walk in the sun, look at the birds and trees and just relax. But of course, Kevin had different plans for me and the family. We were going to cut bale strings that afternoon. That was a task where you cut away the twine that holds together the thousand-pound bales that we have on the farm. First you have to cut through the strings with a knife, and then you wind them up to throw away, because they are a danger if left on the ground. The cows can get hold of them if they aren't wrapped up properly, and try to eat them. If they get caught under a wheel, they can get wrapped up around the axles. Ava and Kierra usually do about twenty to forty a week. Of course, you have to do the work when the sun is shining and it is warm. Since Ava, Brant, and I were all at home, this weekend was the perfect opportunity.

Some of the bales were really old, and the twine was very tight, so as you pulled the string, a lot of the hay came with it. When the wind was blowing the right way (or the wrong way, as it were) it whipped all the hay into your face, eyes, ears, and hair. Even if you were wearing a jacket zipped to the top, the hay would still get all the way into your clothes, all the way down to your chest. So, let's just say I was grouchy. I had wanted to go for a walk and now I was doing this.

Then it started. Ava and Brant were fighting over this, that, and everything. Ava lost her knife, Brant got stuck with the ATV and there was a fight over how to get it out. My brain was on some kind of *where the fuck am I??* vibe, and as I turned my head, Brant ran the ATV into Ava's ATV. She was yelling and he was yelling. Everyone was ok but by then, I just wanted to start crying.

At that point, I heard Kevin's voice saying, "Next year when Ava isn't here, Michelle, this will be your new job."

That did it! How dare he talk to me like I was one of the kids, or a hired hand, or someone who had nothing else to do? I just couldn't say out loud what I was thinking.

What a great plan, Kevin! I was just thinking how I needed something to do. I work my own job, make all the meals, do all the shopping, buy all the gifts, make all the appointments, do all the cleaning, laundry, plan all the vacations, pack the camper, make photo books, do the taxes, take Brant to soccer...you're right! I would be the perfect choice for that position. Who the fuck needs yoga and meditation anyway? I'll write in my gratitude journal while I'm cutting bale strings that I am so grateful I didn't kill myself or shit in my pants today. I'm thankful for hot water so I can pull out all the hay out of my ears, nose and in between my boobs. This is perfect! Therapy, exercise, and gratitude all done for the week in one fell swoop.

Things went south from that point on. Tears started to flow down my cheeks, and I told Brant to drive me back to the house. I didn't know where I was going, but I was going far away from this yard. I told him very nicely that Mom needed a little time out because she was having trouble with mindfulness. She needed to rest, and to tell Dad and Ava that I was ok, but I just needed a time out.

When we got to the house, I got into my own car and took off my Carhartts that were covered in hay, molasses and cow poop, but I left the straw in my hair and down my boobs and I started driving. Crying, crying, crying, wanting to run away but not knowing where to go, I decided to drive to a neighboring city and then possibly stay in a hotel there. Maybe I would try to calm down first by buying myself a journal and a pen from Dollarama and going to sit in Starbucks and write down just why I was so angry. I calmed down then, and finally felt well enough to head back home. I bought them some fried chicken from Mary Brown's as a peace offering for dinner.

I had a couple of things to say to them all after dinner. What happened next was a kind of breakthrough for me, and my tech told me later that it was a big step and that I should see it as a great achievement. I told them how I felt, how their actions made me feel, and how I wanted to set some boundaries with them.

"One thing is that I need everyone to be kinder," I said. My emotions were very high and I started to cry. "I need everyone here to take their chaos down a notch, because I can't take it." I paused and took a deep breath. "I need everyone to be kinder and more patient with each other."

After I spoke, I felt so much lighter, like a weight was gone. And nothing terrible happened. On the contrary, the kids were very sympathetic and concerned, and it ended up being a very calm and healthy conversation.

Kevin's and my story is a little more complicated. After the kids went to their rooms, I got him to sit facing me on the rug and I looked him dead in the eyes.

"There have been some things bothering me and I wanted to address those face to face," I began.

I had never in thirty years done that before and let me tell you, it was effective. He saw into my eyes while I was talking, and I saw into his, and there was nowhere to hide for either of us.

I always thought my violent thoughts of self-harm were only when I felt I had screwed something up, drafted an email wrong, forgot the library books, missed writing an appointment down, or when I looked at the cottage cheese in the mirror. Truth is today I discovered it wasn't just then, it was the times I never said what I meant. I never walked my own walk, I never told someone they did in fact hurt me, because I had sworn to myself, I wouldn't be that sensitive, poor me person. I have it so ingrained in my head that I want to be the opposite and am accountable only for how I interpret things that if I do get hurt, I take it out on myself. In some ways it is like smiling and saying everything is good and then packing it in to go along with my other thoughts of self-hate. I have gotten so good at being polite and not showing any upset emotion that people believe I am always happy, good natured and easy going. Problem with that is I'm damaging myself on the inside because I take the hurt that I got from someone, and I turn it towards another reason to hate myself.

Say what you mean, mean what you say.

So I will say that I am progressing. Some days are shit, some are okay, and some are great. I feel like I am building my foundation so that we can live together in harmony, not like on *The Bachelor* with roses and fireworks, but as a real family, with proper communication, understanding, and awareness that we are all getting our needs met. We are taking it one day at a time.

Final thoughts

I went to my new therapist today and she asked me the same question that I wrote about a lot in this book, "Why do you hate yourself so much?" I knew there were lots of deep-seated reasons, and we talked about depression and some other issues. But I said to her that one of the main reasons I hated myself was because I felt like a sham. I felt like a con artist. I fooled everyone for too many years and I hated myself for it.

I told her about an exchange employee we had one year from Uganda. Her name was Hawa, and I volunteered to host her at our farm. I knew the girls would love hearing about Africa, as would I and Kevin. I thought of it as a good growth opportunity for us all.

She was in absolute awe of everything we had.

She said repeatedly, "You are such a lucky woman; your husband is not lazy like mine. I kiss his feet in the morning and make his breakfast before I go to work while he sits and drinks all day."

She also told me, "Your society has thrived while ours is broken down. Our houses look like the mud homes you had in the early 1900s. We never progressed, but you did."

Our conversations always centered around how lucky I was – to have been born in this country, to have income, to own land, to be part of a loving extended family, and to take yearly vacations. She thought I was the perfect Barbie with the perfect Ken with the dreamhouse, and she thought I took it for granted.

Well the truth is I do take it for granted, as I think most of us in Canada do. How different my life would have been if I had been born in Uganda. She gave me and the kids a huge dose of reality. I cried when she left, knowing she was going back to days of not having enough money to even give her girls tea for breakfast, never mind food. I felt so guilty for all that we had and all that we wasted. I felt guilty that she didn't even know how unhappy I was. I hated myself and the constant violent images being thrown at me. I hated how I hid it all and put up a big smile and a laugh. In her eyes I had everything in the world, but in my eyes, not only did I not feel happy, or appreciative, or lucky, I felt empty. I was like one of those dolls that laughs when you pull the string on her back, but is hollow inside.

It felt almost like double guilt – guilt that I took my world for granted and guilt that I couldn't stand my own skin living in this world I took for granted. How awful! Poor little rich girl! I needed to stop feeling sorry for myself and get out of bed and make her proud. I should make her see that I appreciated the life I was handed. For goodness' sake, in her eyes I was as rich as J-Lo! If I were at J-Lo's house, I certainly would want her to appreciate it and not whine about how sad she was and how she hated herself.

But that wasn't fair. If I were in a wheelchair with a physical illness, she would have had empathy for me and seen how hard I worked. But as I've said, there is no empathy for someone who has an invisible disability. At least I never had any for myself. I never gave myself the grace to say, "I really don't feel well this week. I can't host a birthday party, go on a work trip, vaccinate cows, take the kids to the lake." I never gave myself those options.

Some people would say, "Well, at least you didn't whine about it and feel sorry for yourself. You carried on like we all do and kept quiet about it. A lot of people have it worse than you."

But it wasn't just that I didn't feel sorry for myself. It was that I hated myself for the persona I had created. I was so worried about what everyone would think of me, I didn't ever stop to think of myself.

What do I think of me? I think for the first time in my life, I am not a facade, I am me. I am the same person described above, but I am free. I'm finally free of my deep dark secret, free to keep living the exact way I have been, but now being honest, being real, and being comfortable in my own skin.

***

My name is Michelle Temple and I have harm OCD with violent imagery and depression. I have endometriosis and ischemic colitis. I am getting better but I will have ups and downs based on life's stressful events that cannot be avoided. I need to take better care of myself and my illnesses.

I am a successful chartered accountant, manager, farm wife, mother, daughter, sister, friend. I love the outdoors, gorgeous sunsets, hikes, the lake, the ocean, a fire, a hot tub, coffee in a real mug, travelling, talking about passionate subjects, playing games, laughing and having fun! Oh, and I write now too!

I am going to learn to forgive myself.

I have learned that my self hate has perpetuated my OCD violent image symptoms. Whenever I would see a violent image, I would hate myself more. Every time I pushed down the hate, I had more images. It was a cycle of hate, guilt, and shame.

I am not educated in mental health, but if you find anything resonating with you – self-image, weight, OCD in any form, eating, contamination, germs, hoarding, compulsive shopping, gambling, anxiety, depression, addiction in any form, any mental illness – just know that you are not alone. You probably hate yourself more every time symptoms happen, and my advice is to get help. But first you have to forgive yourself. You can start to heal anything when you put on your oxygen mask first.

So this is our collective to do list:

Let's see how far we can make it if we start loving and accepting ourselves.

Let's forgive ourselves for all the mental and physical illnesses; our souls and our power are above it.

Let's embrace every part of ourselves, every broken part. Let's look at the brokenness, look it square in the eyes and tell it that we are stronger than it.

Let's remember that our soul's self-love is going to win, a brain is just a brain, and we are each so much more than our brain and all our physical pieces.

Let's tell our stories and help a friend, and I'll meet you again soon to catch up.

Love,
Michelle

A letter to the scared little girl who doesn't like herself
Hi, cutie,
I know you feel scared right now, and I know how much it worries you that your uncle could hurt you and your family. I know you stay up at night pondering which rooms he will go into and who he will kill first. Mom and Dad first and you second. You're scared for your mom and dad. You wish you could take your mom's pain away. You want her to be happy, as happy as she tries to make you. She doesn't see that you are scared and that is not her fault. But I know you are holding it inside to save her from the worry, and that doesn't help you. Possibly it doesn't help her either, because she never gets to be vulnerable with you and show you that she might have been scared, too. She just does everything she can to protect you. She didn't tell you that, but it's true. She wanted the absolute best for you, and to make everything so much better than her childhood.
You are scared that someday, someone you love will snap and hurt you. You are scared that someday it might be you who hurt people. It's not you. I can tell you now that I have done everything I could to protect you, and we made it. You can rest now knowing that I lived the life you wanted. I had tons of joy, three gorgeous children, a wonderful supportive husband, and a huge support network of friends and family. Mom and Dad are still here, and they still spoil me. They are good, and we all made it. I also know that Aunt Elaine is like a grandma to you. She loves you, teases you, plays lots of games with you, and even had a Cabbage Patch party at her house for you one time. She gives you coffee with tons of sugar and cream so you can be like her. She loves fun like you do. She loves organizing people to play ball outside and to go camping. She loves to be a prankster and start water fights or some type of game to get a rise out of people and get them laughing and having fun.
I'm sorry I never realized what that means to you. I've seen her empty house and all its details in my dreams hundreds of times, but I didn't know you were trying to

show me that the house was empty and lonely without her. Grief has a funny way of coming back years later, but that has allowed me to deal with it for you now. Don't worry; the love you receive from her now and the world that she shows you will live on even after she dies. She is not going anywhere, because she is part of me.

I hope you can stop being scared and know that I have your back, I am strong and I'm going to protect you so that you can live the life of your dreams.

I know you always felt like you were chubby and unlovable at a bigger size. I know in your mind it meant you weren't good enough as you were. I'm sorry you internalized these things to mean that you weren't pretty enough. Unfortunately, all the words became your internal voice and your internal critic.

You can let that go now. You will grow up and have a wonderful husband who loves you the way you are. Your mom and dad have always loved you the way you are. Your friends and family unconditionally love every piece of you. They don't want you to be any different. They only wish you peace and happiness. You can let go of the thoughts that you aren't enough just as you are. Please know that your body did amazing things. It carried three beautiful babies, it skied, it climbed mountains, it walked through sunsets, it kayaked on water that was like glass, it played horsie and airplane with your kids. It did everything that matters.

I know you feel stupid and I'm not sure why. You think you say the wrong things and you think others will think you're stupid. I'm not sure where those thoughts started, but I want you to know it's not true. You will be successful; you will write one of the hardest exams over four days and you will pass on your first try. You love learning things about the world around you, you are inquisitive and passionate about places in the world, the magic of your body, science, and religion. You excel at empathy. You always put yourself in someone else's shoes and treat people kindly. You no longer have to say you're dumb or stupid, you have proven that you are not, and you have so much to offer to those around you. You help them just as they help you.

I love you. I love your zest for life. I love that you enjoy all the little things, like the lake, the campfire, being with your family, laughing, dancing, and listening to music. I love everything about who you are. You're a sweet, fun, kid…a little lazy on the cleaning but hey, you gotta have some faults, right? You know what is important and if you have to choose between cleaning the bathroom or playing with the kids at the sand dunes, hands down you will always choose the sand dunes. Your kids will thank you for that. You created a place for them that you would have loved at your age, travelling, camping, beach time, canoeing, hiking, hot tubbing…you gave this all to them. Thank you. Thank you for being you and I will help you remember the positives of when you grew up.

Love,
Me, in forty-eight years

www.ingramcontent.com/pod-product-compliance
Lightning Source LLC
Chambersburg PA
CBHW052145070526
44585CB00017B/1990